Nalini Rajan is Dean of Studies and Professor, Asian College of Journalism, Chennai. She has taken classes on secularism for her students over 20 years. She has a doctorate in Social Communication, specializing in political philosophy, from the Catholic University of Louvain, Belgium. She has travelled widely and held post-doctoral fellowships in the Universities of Oxford and Edinburgh, and in New York. She has written five books on political philosophy, including *The Story of Secularism: 15th–21st Century* and *Religious Faith, Ideology, Citizenship: The View from Below* (co-author), three works of fiction, and edited six volumes on media studies. Her first novel, *The Pangolin's Tale*, was long-listed for the 2007 Man Asian Literary Prize. She is General Editor of the series, *Studies in Journalism* (Orient Blackswan).

SECULARISM

How India Reshaped the Idea

Nalini Rajan

SPEAKING
TIGER

SPEAKING TIGER BOOKS LLP
125A, Ground Floor, Shahpur Jat, near Asiad Village,
New Delhi 110049

First published by Speaking Tiger Books 2024

ISBN: 978-93-5447-671-6
eISBN: 978-93-5447-672-3

10 9 8 7 6 5 4 3 2 1

Typeset in Garamond Premier Pro by SÜRYA, New Delhi
Printed at HT Media Ltd, Greater Noida

CONTENTS

Introduction

Harsh Mander

This is the third in a series of short books on the Indian Constitution that we have tried to bring together to inform the debates—sometimes bitter and not so well-informed—about the core ideas of the Constitution. Even among the ideas of the Constitution that are being contested today, the most rancorous debates centre on the idea of secularism.

At the time of India's freedom, the world was still rebuilding and healing from the devastation and wounds left by the Second World War. The Holocaust had left around six million Jews, two-thirds of the entire Jewish people in Europe, dead, many in gas chambers built in Nazi Germany, the state led by Adolf Hitler from 1933 to 1945; along with multitudes of Roma and Sinti people, homosexual men, persons with disability and prisoners of war. The people of the world were learning from this horrific and tragic genocide the dangers of what happens in a country if minorities—religious, racial, ethnic, caste, sexual—are not protected. They were learning the cataclysmic consequences of the politics of hate and division. These were also lessons for the Indian people. The same lessons came out of the horrific Partition riots, and from India's epic freedom struggle.

Although the word 'secularism' was added to the Preamble only in the mid-70s, it was central to the politics and morality of the Constitution as drafted and adopted by the Constituent Assembly. Therefore, its omission from the version of the Constitution that was given to every member of Parliament when the new Parliament building was inaugurated in 2023 was rightly criticized.

This is not to deny the fact that the inclusion of secularism in India's Constitution has been both debated and attacked from the time of the writing of the Constitution, from both the left and the right. Some believe that the idea of secularism is a Western idea that grew from the particular histories of contestations of power between the church and the state, and therefore sits uneasily in India with its very distinct history and civilizational experience. Others, from the right, have attacked what they describe sometimes as 'pseudo-secularism' and sometimes as 'minority appeasement' for the alleged Muslim vote bank. Lal Krishna Advani, one of the co-founders of the Bharatiya Janata Party, argues that India needs 'genuine' secularism, which for him is embodied in the ideology and practice, oddly enough, of Hindutva!

Nalini Rajan, who has been teaching her students the ideas of secularism for two decades, confronts the many contestations and debates to affirm the Indian idea of secularism around the triage of ideas of state neutrality towards all religions, equal citizenship and religious freedom. She also speaks of the inherent tensions between these ideas. Even as the deviations in the practice of almost every political party and most governments since Independence and many significant court judgements reveal the faultlines with respect to secularism, this does not change the reality that the idea of secularism is inseparable from the idea of the inclusive and just India our founders had sought to build.

India's Struggle for Freedom

Mahatma Gandhi returned to India from the distant shores of South Africa in 1915. He was forty-five years old. The India he returned to, not unlike the one he had left as a young man, was mired in many unfreedoms, the primary one for a great many being political, enslaved as India was to rulers from across the seas for nearly two lightless centuries.

The colonial government could throw for years into prison people who rallied or fought against their rule. Some were hung from the gallows like the heroic young revolutionary, Bhagat Singh, some were banished for lifetimes to the distant Andaman Islands. Even those committed to peaceful, non-violent resistance to foreign rule were beaten back and often bundled into jail, sometimes for long periods of time.

The British colonized India because, at the time they arrived, this was one of the wealthiest and most industrialized countries in the world. In the two centuries of their rule, most industries had been destroyed, farming starved through rack-renting and artisans impoverished. There was misery and hunger in the famine-ravished countryside. The average lifespan of a common Indian was as low as 21 years at the time when Gandhiji returned to India.

All colonized people found their own pathways to freedom, like the proud people of India who rose heroically in revolt. What marks out our freedom struggle from most others, however, was that the mainstream of our struggle was founded on the pivotal moral idea of *ahimsa*, or non-violence. Ahimsa means the resolve that I will fight you for my freedom and dignity, resolutely, accepting whatever consequences this battle will extract from me, including a bullet or banishment to prison; but even as I struggle against you for what is right and just, I will never hate you, and I will wish or cause you no injury or harm.

A Broken, Wounded India

The British eventually bent to the resilience of this struggle. However, they left not one but two nations—India and Pakistan. In frenzied riots on both sides of the new border which now suddenly separated sister from sister and brother from brother, a madness of hate seized the sub-continent. Hindus, Muslims and Sikhs slaughtered each other with a viciousness that cast a very dark and long shadow on the celebrations of freedom. Estimates of mortality range up to two million; an uncounted number were raped and abducted. Fourteen million people were cruelly uprooted from their homes, travelling often on foot, weary and heartbroken, for hundreds of kilometres, with their small children and the few belongings that they had been able to salvage on their aching backs. There is only one other distress migration, which humankind has witnessed in the course of recorded history, that was larger than this one. This was the forced trafficking of Africans as slaves to the Americas.

Pakistan was created as an independent nation for the Muslim people who lived in the west and east flanks of the teeming country. Its leaders urged Muslims in other parts of India to move to Pakistan to make this new nation their home.

There were some who advocated that India should be a country *only* for the Hindus—a Hindu India, a mirror image of a Muslim Pakistan. This would be a fitting reply to Pakistan, they felt, and would secure justice to India's overwhelming Hindu majority.

But Gandhiji had led our freedom struggle on the shining promise that India would be a country where people of every religion (or no religion!), caste, language and gender would be equal citizens in every way. Jawaharlal Nehru, India's first prime minister, declared that India would belong equally to all those who chose to make this their home, irrespective of their religion or community. One of Gandhi's closest associates, Maulana Azad, often spoke glowingly of his great pride, sense of ownership and resolute belonging to this country which he so loved. He declared that he was Muslim *and* he was Indian, and both these identities were inseparable from him, that he was willing to give up neither of these. He said India had given a great deal to its Muslim people, and the Muslim people too had given a great deal to their country. On 23 October 1947, as the country was reeling under the Partition, he stood tall on the ramparts of the grand Jama Masjid in Delhi and made a historic, heartfelt appeal to Muslims living in various parts of India to stay on, because this was their country and would always be.

This call was echoed over and over again by a Gandhi devastated to his soul by the tumult of religious hate and violence in India and Pakistan. He entreated Muslims over and over again to stay on in an India that he pledged would belong equally, in every way, to its Muslim citizens. A very large number of Muslims heeded his call, and the call of Maulana Azad and Jawaharlal Nehru, opting for multi-faith India over Muslim Pakistan.

When India was celebrating freedom in August 1947, however, Mahatma Gandhi was not in Delhi to celebrate as the Union Jack was lowered and the Indian Tricolour raised. He was instead in Calcutta, where Muslims and

Hindus were killing each other in what appeared to be an unending bloodbath of hate. He went on an epic fast refusing to eat a morsel of food until the last of the violence had ended. He returned then to Delhi, trying to quell the hate and violence of hundreds of thousands of angry and sullen refugees separated forever from their homeland in what was now Pakistan. (These included my own extended family, uprooted from their birthplace.) He had planned then to travel (pointedly without a visa) into Pakistan to try to douse the fires of hatred that raged in this newly born country. But this was not to be.

Every day, Mahatma Gandhi would hold a prayer meeting, in which he recited prayers from all major religions. One of his favourite hymns included the line: '*Ishwar-Allah tero naam*'. On a winter evening on 30 January 1948, on his way to his prayer meeting, he was killed by a man violently opposed to his idea of an India which would belong equally to all people of all faiths. A stricken people mourned the death of the father of the nation, a man who paved the path to building a country which was humane and inclusive, which assured equal rights as citizens to people of every religion, caste, language and gender.

Babasaheb Ambedkar, who would lead the writing of India's Constitution, had warned that any attempt to restrict India to people of the majority Hindu faith would be a 'calamity' for the nation and for democracy.

As the bullets of Gandhi's assassin signalled, not everyone shared this vision for India.

The Constitution—a Dream, a Vision, a Set of Promises

Centuries of colonial bondage had reduced India from one of the wealthiest to one of the poorest countries of the world, in which famine, illiteracy, sickness and want stalked the countryside. For millennia, the cruel system of caste had made life a living hell for those unfortunate enough to be born into disadvantaged castes. Women were denied rights to property, education, work and dignity, and even sometimes life itself.

Would we change all of this, and how? Who would this country belong to? Who would govern this country? How would the rulers be chosen? What powers would these rulers have? What powers and rights would the people have? And would the country's minorities—religious, caste, tribal and gender—be protected?

It was answers to questions like these that were written into the Constitution of newly independent India.

What is a constitution? It is a dream, a vision, a set of promises; a compendium of guarantees, a store-house of aspirations. It is a solemn articulation of the values that the country will hold close to its collective soul in its journey in the decades and centuries which lie ahead. It is the collective imagination of the destination which the country pledges to reach.

Most constitutions, except for those in the United Kingdom, Israel, Saudi Arabia and a few others, are written documents. The Constitution of India was written by a collective, the Constituent Assembly. They sat in the grand historic circular building which became for over seven decades the Parliament of the Indian republic. The Constituent Assembly had over three hundred members. These women and men were, in a sense, the founding mothers and fathers of the Constitution. They were drawn from the people elected into the provincial assemblies of the time. And about a third were nominated, to ensure that those in attendance included people of every religion, caste, gender, culture, community and profession. The Constituent Assembly did not have members only from the Congress party which led India to freedom; members were invited even from parties strongly opposed to the Congress. One example is Babasaheb Bhimrao Ambedkar, who was the brave, charismatic and inspiring leader of the Scheduled Castes Federation, who had often stood in stout opposition to the Congress led by Gandhiji. Members of the Hindu Right were also invited to sit in the Constituent Assembly. There were many small kingdoms which were merged into the Indian nation, and their representatives were also members of this assembly.

Looking back today, we realize that it should have had many more women, more persons with disability, more Adivasi and Dalit people, many more working poor people, from factories and farms, and more gender minorities. But there's no denying the fact that the fine women and men who sat on the benches of the Constituent Assembly did indeed speak for all the people of India.

The first sittings of the Constituent Assembly began even before India became free, in the winter of 1946. The assembly deliberated for three years. A smaller group was carved out of the assembly called the Drafting Committee, which worked on the detailed draft of the constitution, and each of the sections of this draft were discussed in the assembly and then put to vote.

The chairperson of this drafting committee was one of the most learned men in the assembly, Dr Ambedkar, affectionately called Babasaheb. He contributed invaluably to many of the progressive measures written into our constitution. He was born into a very poor family of a soldier in the Indian army, from one of the most oppressed castes. On people from these castes for centuries was inflicted the most cruel form of discrimination which we know as untouchability. (Shamefully, that and many such practices endure in free India.) The country is fortunate that such a man—highly educated, wise and one who knew from personal experience the suffering of the most oppressed of our people—led the process of writing the Constitution. The two women members of the Drafting Committee, Hansa Mehta and Rajkumari Amrit Kaur, contributed spiritedly and thoughtfully to the deliberations, seeking to make the Constitution also reflect the aspirations of the forgotten and oppressed half of the population, women.

We owe a lot to the founding mothers and fathers of the Constitution, who drew with us and for us the contours of the dream and the promise of a country based on equality and humanity which we resolved to build, one day.

From Mahatma Gandhi, we imbibed the idea and practice of radical love. From Babasaheb Ambedkar we learned the idea and practice of radical equality. These together became the cornerstones of our Constitution.

Hum Log: We, the People of India

Who indeed gave to us our constitution? The opening lines of the document answer this question. They tell us that 'We, the people of India' ('*Hum, Bharat ke log*') gave to ourselves this constitution. Who are 'we, the people of India'? We are the people who lived in this great and ancient land in past centuries; we are the people who were alive in India when the Constitution was framed; and we are the people of generations which followed and are still to follow. 'We' includes our grandparents and parents, it includes each of us who reside in this vast terrain today. And 'we' will include our children and their children one day.

The 'we' in 'we, the people' is the ocean in which many, many different little streams and mighty rivers meet. We derive strength and vitality from the plurality of our magnificent heritage. This kaleidoscope of our diversity is mirrored in our ever-changing natural features—from the Himalayas to the rivers, the forests to the deserts, the deltas to the plateaus, the coastlines to the islands. This kaleidoscope is made up of our music, of our art, of our dance forms, of our *gharanas* of classical music, and of their vibrant intermingling fusions. Of the spectacular range of our culinary choices, our varied taste buds that create a plethora of platters and cuisines, changing every few hundred miles. Of every festival of every religion and culture, which in our land becomes an Indian festival. Of our thousands of dialects and languages, such that if two people are selected at random from any ten in our country, chances are that they will speak different tongues.

India is the glorious symphony of our many different voices. It is a wondrous palette in which you can find every colour in the world, and we are privileged to be able to draw paintings of our lives from this multitude of colours.

All of these, all and every one of us, you and I, make 'we, the people'.

The Preamble

The soul of the Constitution, its essence, is contained in a single page, which is called the Preamble. Every religion has a holy book, and prayer. Some people say that for the people of India, our holy book is our Constitution, and our prayer the Preamble.

But holy books are often placed on an unreachable pedestal; holy books cannot be questioned or changed. The Constitution is not that kind of holy book. It is a book which belongs to we, the people of India, one that protects and guides us through difficult times, but one that can be discussed, challenged and also collectively changed. It is a book of the people, not of the gods. It contains within it the values that the people of India pledge to uphold as the nation is built and as later generations come and go.

A Sovereign Democratic Republic

The preamble first talks of the kind of country India will be. India will be sovereign, it says. This means its destiny will no longer be controlled by any foreign power. It will be democratic. This means its government will be chosen by its people. It will be a republic, which means that the ruler will not be born into power, in the way kings and queens have been born for centuries. Nor will the ruler snatch power through the bloodshed and brute force of military conquest or coups. The ruler will have to be elected by the people. Anyone, including those born into the greatest disadvantage, will have the right to aspire to become rulers, and seek the support of the people for the right to rule them.

An important question arose before the Constituent Assembly about which people should have the right to vote for their government. India became the first of the newly independent countries to give *every* person—man, woman or transgender, rich or poor, educated or uneducated—exactly equal political power to choose their rulers. One person, one vote. The richest and the most powerful man in the country would have the same single vote as the poorest, most destitute trans woman. A young person born in India today may think this is the most normal thing to do, but it wasn't at the time. It was a brave and radical—and some would say, audacious—idea. In Western democracies, for a long time only white men of wealth enjoyed the right to vote. Women had to fight long for an equal right to vote. In the United States of America, for instance, women got the right to vote only in 1920, and African Americans only in 1965. In Australia, aboriginal Australians did not get the right to vote until 1962. In India, the idea of universal suffrage for every person was adopted without any noteworthy dissent.

Many people had feared that Indians were not ready for this radical system of voting rights for all people, called universal adult franchise. Less than one in five people were even literate at the time of Independence; among women there were less than one in ten. But our founding mothers and fathers still resolved to place their faith in the ordinary Indian, even those denied education, wealth and social standing. They ensured that they would be guaranteed as their birth-right the opportunity to participate equally with every other Indian, the most wealthy, educated, socially or politically powerful, in choosing their governments, and through this, in building the nation and their collective destinies. For a society that would not allow the 'lower' castes to step inside schools and temples, to possess land, and to live with dignity; for a society that would not allow some women even the chance to be born, let alone to own and inherit property and to work shoulder to shoulder with men—for this society to resolve to ensure the same and equal right to vote for every person, though not the end of the road, was a truly iridescent beginning to the great adventure of building a new nation.

From the first election in India in 1951, people from around the world watched with wonder and admiration as impoverished people, disadvantaged castes and women formed the longest lines outside polling booths. This has remained unchanged even until today. India's people of disadvantage are found to choose carefully and thoughtfully. The wonderment is that the people democracy has most let down are those who continue to have the greatest faith in this same democracy.

Socialist and Secular

The Preamble goes on to mandate that the country will be socialist. This means many things. That the government must be committed to ensuring a decent standard of living for all its citizens. It must protect them from hunger and joblessness, and ensure equal and affordable education, health care, housing, decent work and social protection to all. It means a conscious state resolve to prevent the concentration of wealth in a few hands.

The Preamble also lays down that India will be a secular country. This means that the government will have no religion, and it will neither practise nor promote any particular religion. It will not discriminate in any way between people on the basis of their religion, whether they form a tiny minority of people, numbering not more than a few hundred people, following their traditional faith, or those who follow the religion of the largest majority of the Indian people. It also means that the state will promote harmony and goodwill between people with different belief systems.

In a particularly significant judgement of the Delhi High Court which decriminalized homosexuality in 2006, despite the stout opposition of people of almost every religious faith in the country, the bench declared that India's secular constitution gives every citizen of the country the freedom to follow their faith and beliefs. Of course, if their moral rules contradict the morality of the Constitution, it is constitutional morality that must prevail over individual religious beliefs. This ruling was first overturned by the Supreme Court, and then restored, but sexual minorities are still denied the equal right of people of the same sex to marry.

Justice

The Constitution promises equal justice to all people, in all aspects of their lives. Justice here does not simply mean what goes on in the courts. It means fairness. It means that people will not face discrimination in society because of their religion, caste, gender, sexuality or disability. They will not face discrimination in their participation in the economy, in work and in the markets. Women and men (and gay and trans people) will have equal access to employment, based only on their merit and not their gender, and will get equal pay for equal work. The ancient system of *begar*, or forced labour, imposed mostly on the most disadvantaged castes was abolished by the Constitution. No one could be kept as a bonded labourer. All persons are also to be treated fairly in their political life, when they go out to vote, to campaign, or to fight elections.

Liberty

One of the most important promises of the Constitution is of liberty, or freedom. In many protests around the country, slogans are raised for *azaadi*. Azaadi means liberty or freedom. What kinds of freedom or azaadi does the Constitution guarantee? It mandates freedom of thought, expression and belief. This means that every citizen is free to think, speak and believe in ideas which may not conform to the views of the government in power, or of the majority of people. In other words, it grants the freedom of conscience, the freedom to dissent, to disagree with power—political, social and economic power. Many believe that this freedom lies at the core of democracy.

The right to dissent must also carry the freedom from fear, the assurance that I will not be punished for holding beliefs different from those of the powerful. Rabindranath Tagore speaks glowingly of such a country, in which 'the mind is without fear, and the head is held high...' History stands witness that it was only when brave women and men raised their voices against established orthodoxies of their time—when Galileo said the world was round and not flat, or when Savitribai Phule and Fatima Sheikh established schools for girls when the kitchen was believed to be the only fitting confine for women, when Raja Ram Mohan Roy railed against a woman being burnt on her husband's pyre for *sati* or children being tied in marriage, when Babasaheb Ambedkar fought the idea and practice of caste in which the accident of your birth determines all your life chances, condemning you to a life of humiliation and discrimination, barring you from education and dignified work—that the world became a better place for later generations. We are here today because they refused to conform. Conformity leads to deadwood and regression. The freedom of conscience, the freedom to dissent, is therefore central to the pledge of liberty for all, which our constitution guarantees.

The Constitution also importantly assures the freedom of faith and worship. It protects the right of every person to follow her religion, her forms of worship, her ways of life including her choice of food and clothes. It allows people not just to follow but also to propagate their faith, and to establish their religious institutions.

There are other vital freedoms as well which are mandated by our constitution. These include the freedom to pursue the occupation we choose, to move to any part of the country and to form associations or unions, to write and produce art, poetry, novels, books, philosophy, theatre, films—and video games and Instagram videos—which reflect our belief systems and our creativity.

Equality

There are many ways that we are not equal. Some of us run faster than others, some cook better, some sing or dance or paint better, some score better marks in class, some can become mothers and others cannot, and so on. But above all of these differences, the Constitution recognizes us all to be equal in a fundamental way: we are equal in human dignity and human worth. There is, from this yardstick, no difference between the wealthiest person and someone begging for alms outside a temple or dargah. It is because of this inherent intrinsic equality that we all have an equal vote and equal rights and freedoms.

The Constitution requires that the government should ensure equality of opportunity. This means that wherever you might be born, in a village, a slum, the city streets or a mansion, you are entitled to the same opportunities to study, in the same quality school or college, and the same chances to develop your potential, whether for intellectual pursuit, sports, music, art or anything else. It also requires governments to ensure equality of status. This is an even more difficult task. It means that at least to some degree, governments must ensure more equal conditions of life to those who are more disadvantaged. This can only be done by what is called redistribution, by taxing the wealthy to ensure the right to a decent life to the disadvantaged; and by reservations or affirmative action, which recognizes that people who have for centuries been treated unequally need special support in education and jobs for them to achieve real equality in the conditions of their lives.

The Constitution also firmly and categorically bans the practice of untouchability. This—along with the principle of one person, one vote—are arguably the most radical sections of the Constitution. It outlaws unambiguously a practice that has brutalized and shamed Indian society for at least two millennia. Untouchability is one of the most troubling, cruel and disgraceful parts of India's historical legacy. By the accident of birth into a particular caste, it condemns people to a life where they are not allowed into religious shrines, share food or water with other people who will avoid so much as their touch, and will prevent them from walking on the same road as them or riding a horse in a wedding procession, or studying in school or college. The Constitution prohibited these shameful practices. This provision transforms the Constitution, at least in part, into a luminous moral document, seeking to confront and atone for the crimes of our history.

Fraternity

Fraternity in English means brotherhood. This must of course include sisterhood as well. The Hindi version of the Constitution uses the beautiful word *bandhuta*. Derived from Sanskrit, this means the idea that we are bound to and with each other. Looking at it in another way, *bandhu* means friend, so bandhuta can also be understood as an ideology of friendship.

Fraternity or bandhuta encompasses the lustrous idea that we might have between us enormous differences—of wealth, gender, caste, religion, language, ability, the colour of our skins, the size of our eyes and noses, who we choose to love and marry, the food we eat, the clothes we wear, and so much else—but are *bound to and with each other* despite that. We are brothers, sisters, friends.

Dr Ambedkar rightly said that the most important idea in the Constitution is the idea of fraternity. It is this idea which affirms the equal dignity of every individual. We learn from him that the other foundational ideas of the Constitution can be conceivably accomplished even if there is no fraternity. But this would be possible only by enforcing these through the strong arm of the state. However, if there is fraternity in society, then you don't need the state to enforce justice, liberty, equality: instead, these become the natural order of things.

Bandhuta is therefore the single most precious idea of the Constitution, but also the hardest to accomplish. So many people teach us hate—our leaders, our peers, our elders, our heroes from films and sports, our friends. We need instead teachers, leaders, philosophers, writers, film-makers, singers, artists, friends and family who teach us love.

Remember, it is not a country founded on hate, fear, division and inequality which we, the people of India promised to build. The country we gave to ourselves was a humane and equal country founded on love. Bandhuta is what brings us together as one country. We are not one country because we are alike. We are one country because, despite every difference in the way we look, eat, dress, speak, worship, love and think, we belong to and with each other. If there are shackles on your feet, I feel my freedom has been stolen. If you sleep hungry, I am unable to sleep. If your suffer loss and pain, tears well up in my eyes.

Our Reality

But what is our reality? Look around. It is apparent that 'we, the people of India' have built a country still far distant from the India we promised ourselves in our constitution. And in some ways this distance is only growing.

Think of which of the magnificent and solemn pledges that we made to ourselves have been realized. What has become of the dreams of our founding mothers and fathers?

A great deal has indeed been accomplished. Every person in this country continues to hold the power to choose her government. Citizens of a large majority of newly independent countries were denied or lost this power, to military coups and dictators. Fewer people in our country are poor, fewer sleep hungry than when we won our freedom. The average length of life has risen from 37 years in 1947 to 67 years three quarters of a century later. We have some fine institutions for teaching the humanities, engineering, medicine and management, our warehouses are overloaded with food grains, we are the IT back office of the world, and our cities glitter with gated colonies, luxury cars and crowded malls.

But look carefully, and you will find that one in every third child is still malnourished. This means that their bodies and brains are not allowed to develop to full potential for lack of nutritious food and clean water. Children of the poor study in separate, significantly less resourced schools than children of the rich. Many are not allowed to study at all, and instead parents still feel compelled to send them out to hard labour. Every second woman is anaemic. Eight out of ten doctors in India work for for-profit private hospitals, and government spending on health care in India is among the lowest in the world. If poor people fall ill, they cannot rely on good quality publicly provisioned health care. Wealth accumulates in an incredibly small numbers of hands, and this is barely taxed. At the other far end of the spectrum, nine out of ten workers toil in casual, insecure, unsafe jobs at dirt wages. As they age, most have barely enough pensions to secure their aging with dignity and health care.

People still suffer horrible violence and discrimination because of their religion, caste and gender; or because they walk the paths of equality that is their right; or when they choose to love and marry outside the socially prescribed boundaries of religion, caste and gender. Adivasis are dispossessed by large powerful corporations from their forests and homelands, and are branded as Maoists and jailed when they protest. Crowds gather and lynch Muslim and Dalit men, beating them to death, and proudly videograph these crimes and circulate these on social media. Untouchability continues with pitiless and ferocious violence. Dalits are beaten and killed in India even today for growing a moustache, for building a two-storied house, for asking for fair wages, for just advancing in life through their own hard work and talent; their children thrashed for drinking water from an earthen pot meant for their 'high-caste' teacher. And these horrific crimes are rarely punished.

Governments punish instead people who disagree with them. The freedom to dissent is dying, with fear and official targeting choking voices of truth. The freedom of religious faith is threatened by the politics of majoritarian hate. People spend years in prison because they are too poor to afford legal counsel, because the courts are clogged and uncaring, because they belong to stigmatized religious and caste identities, or simply because they dare to challenge the injustices of the state.

Reflect on the essence, the morality, the soul of our

constitution. It is not perfect. With the hindsight of history, there are some things we might want to change. But contained in it are the iridescent dreams we had for this nation when it threw off its chains of slavery. These are the ambitions, the lofty and worthy goals that we, the people set for our country. And since these are promises which we have made unto ourselves, it is for you and I, 'we, the people of India', to rebuild this country into the kind, equal, free and just land imagined by our founding mothers and fathers.

We must build with the bricks of our hearts and minds, of our dreams and our struggles, of our accomplishments and our sacrifices, and I hope, of love.

This Series

India recently celebrated seventy-five years of its Independence. As one small tribute to the Indian freedom struggle, we propose a series of ten books that summarize in simple, accessible language the core values, imagination and pledges of the Constitution. The themes for these books we have been drawn mainly from the Preamble—Secularism, Socialism, Democracy, Justice, Liberty, Equality, Fraternity. In addition, we include the themes Scientific Temper and Federalism; these too are essential to the morality of the Indian Constitution. We are fortunate that the fine minds and hearts who we approached—some senior, some younger—all agreed generously to contribute to this series.

These books draw from the Constituent Assembly debates, and indeed from those that preceded them. Each book also looks at how these ideas evolved in independent India, through court rulings and executive actions. The series also looks at the relevance of these ideas to the challenges of the India of today, the extent to which the state, the polity, the economy and society remain faithful to these ideas, the principal contestations to these ideas, and finally, the ways in which these ideas are important for India's future as a humane, democratic state.

Dr Neera Chandhoke, one of India's leading political scientists, and Distinguished Fellow of the Centre for Equity Studies, consented to help me bring out the series and has also written the opening book for it. Ravi Singh, co-founder of Speaking Tiger and one of India's finest editors, agreed to publish this series. We hope to get these translated into Hindi and other Indian languages as well.

At a time when the morality and pledges of the Constitution are under assault, it is our fervent wish that this small project—an effort to unpack and popularize it—will be useful as resistance, defence and public affirmation of the luminous morality of the founding document of India.

'The natural beneficiary of [the] combination of democratization and secularization was the political and ideological left, and it was in these quarters that the old bourgeois belief in science, reason and progress bloomed.'

—Eric Hobsbawm, *The Age of Empire: 1875–1914*

'A secular state is not anti-religious but exists and survives only when religion is no longer hegemonic. It admits a more general equality between believers and unbelievers. It secures peace not only between different kinds of religious believers but between believers and non-believers. It legally sanctions freedoms for all religions but also freedom from religion itself.'

—Rajeev Bhargava, 'India's Secular Constitution',
in *India's Living Constitution* (2002)

Author's Preface

For social scientists, concepts have a disconcerting way of changing over a long period of time.

As a postdoctoral fellow working on the philosopher John Rawls in the 1990s, I met a professor from my graduate days who urged me to focus on ideas of secularism within the Indian context. At that time, much of my understanding of secularism came from Western sources, and it was not surprising that I parroted many Western notions in my subsequent writing on secularism. While these were useful concepts in themselves, their application was rather limited in the South Asian region.

I think the turning point for me came in 1998, with the publication of Rajeev Bhargava's edited volume, *Secularism and Its Critics*, which I managed to read from cover to cover. It was here that I was exposed to a systematic understanding and critique of secularism of the Indian state, and to that of the hesitant and intermittent secularization of Indian society. After Bhargava's book, of course, there was a tsunami of publications on Indian secularism, on going beyond secularism, and on multiculturalism.

While I acknowledge and thank all the authors of these books, my best teachers really have been my students at the Asian College of Journalism, where I teach secularism as part of an elective course, 'Identities in a Plural Society'. Over the past 20 years or so, students have quizzed, interrogated and challenged me on many of these ideas. As a result, I have understood better the complexity of secularism and have learned to express these ideas more lucidly in writing.

To all the persons who have accompanied me on this long journey of understanding secularism, I owe an immense debt of gratitude. In this process, my ideas have grown far richer and more complex than they were in the 1990s.

A book is always a result of a collaboration between the author, the editors, and the publisher. I am extremely grateful to the initiator of this series on the Indian Constitution, Harsh Mander, for giving me an opportunity to study the fascinating debates and judgements pertaining to the secular clauses in the Constitution and for providing me with very useful feedback on my manuscript. I owe a special debt of gratitude to Neera Chandhoke, co-editor of the series, for her constant support and encouragement. I also thank the publisher, Ravi Singh of Speaking Tiger, for backing all of us in this wonderful project.

Many thanks to Tahira Thapar and Nazeef Mollah for their efforts to make this a better book!

I end with the usual caveat—any mistake in the text is solely my responsibility.

Nalini Rajan
December 2023

Chapter I

Understanding Secularism

Dictionaries and encyclopaedias have a curious way of compressing the meaning of complex terms like 'secularism'.

The Chambers Dictionary defines secularism as 'the belief that the state, morals, education, etc., should be independent of religion'. The Webster Collegiate Dictionary claims that secularism is 'indifference to or rejection or exclusion of religion and religious considerations'. Meanwhile, the Encyclopaedia of Religion and Ethics points out that 'secularism is wholly unconcerned with the unknown world and its interpretation. It deals with the known world, interpreted by experience and neither offers nor forbids any opinion regarding another life'.[1]

These three definitions of secularism seem to call for the separation of state and religion and are simplistic and misleading insofar as they imply that secularism is a single-value idea. As we will see, secularism is a far more complex, triple-value concept. In etymological terms, we find that the word 'secular' is derived from the Latin 'saeculum', which pertains to the length of time equal to the potential lifetime of an individual or that of a new generation. In other words, 'secular' refers to homogeneous, sequential time, as we understand it in today's rational, 'disenchanted'[2] context, and is the antonym of sacred or religious time, which is marked by ritual circularity and seasonal worship.

Historically speaking, in Europe, the 1648 Treaty of Westphalia, which brought an end to the eighty years of strife between Catholic Spain and Protestant Netherlands and Germany, referred to the transfer of Church properties to the monarchy as a process of 'secularization'. Such a transfer of ecclesiastical property to the control of the state also took place in the early phase of the French Revolution, which was officially inaugurated in July 1789, with the storming of the Bastille prison in order to free imprisoned writers and journalists. Of course, the French have their own term for secularism, 'laïcité', which denotes the distinction between the clergy (priests) and the laity (laypersons).

Some sixty years on, in 1851, George Jacob Holyoake formally coined the term 'secularism', while leading a national protest movement in East London. Holyoake defined a secularist as 'one who gives primary attention to those subjects, the issues of which can be tested by the experience of this life. The secularist principle requires that precedence should be given to the duties of this life over those which pertain to another world'.[3] It would seem, then, that Holyoake, too, defined secularism as a separation between the sacred (religious) and the profane (secular) realms, while favouring the latter. There was also an attempt by Holyoake to conflate secularism with notions like science and rationality. The Central Secular Society was founded by Holyoake to encourage people to resort to reasonable thought and action, above all, in their practical, day-to-day life.

John Locke and Toleration

What about the theoretical, or conceptual, way of understanding secularism? One of the earliest theoretical essays on secularism, *A Letter Concerning Toleration*, was written and published by the philosopher John Locke, in 1689. Locke was certainly aware of the sectarian wars in the seventeenth century between Catholics and various sects of Protestants (Anglicans, Lutherans, Calvinists and so on), and he wrote this essay to plead for tolerance towards all religions, even though he had little faith in the Catholic Church as an institution. Locke believed that to tolerate those who differed from us in matters of religion was to abide by the Gospel of Jesus Christ as well as by Reason itself. Locke held the view that earthly judges were not equipped to judge the truth claims of different religions. Even if they were, they could not force anyone to change their religion at will. In matters of religion, neither the monarch nor the state could dictate to people what faith they should choose. Forcing religious homogeneity would lead to far more disorder than allowing diversity of faiths within a polity. Civil government, for Locke, had to be clearly demarcated from all religions. He said, '[T]he Church itself is a thing absolutely separate and distinct from the commonwealth. The boundaries on both sides are fixed and immovable.'[4]

Indeed, Locke expanded the ambit of religious tolerance to include Jews and heathens: 'If a Roman Catholic believes that to be really the body of Christ which another man calls bread, he does no injury to his neighbour. If a Jew do [*sic*] not believe the New Testament to be the Word of God, he does not thereby alter anything in men's civil rights. If a heathen doubt of both Testaments, he is not therefore to be punished as a pernicious citizen.'[5] He goes on to say, '[I] f we may openly speak the truth, and as becomes one man to another, neither Pagan nor Mahometan nor Jew, ought to be excluded from the civil rights of the commonwealth because of his religion.'[6]

Interestingly, Locke does not believe that atheists, who 'deny the being of God', need to be tolerated. He categorically states: 'Promises, covenants, and oaths, which are the bonds of human society, can have no hold upon an atheist.'[7]

So, what are Locke's principal points in *A Letter Concerning Toleration*?

a) The government should be tolerant towards all religions;

b) the government need not be tolerant of atheists;

c) the government should concern itself only with civil matters and should not interfere in the religious preferences of its citizens.

Let us consider the implications of each of these points.

a) What exactly is the scope of religious tolerance? Many kings and queens in various parts of the world have been tolerant towards all religions, to a greater or lesser degree. Here are a few examples of tolerance and intolerance of different sectarian, theocratic rulers.

Let us begin with one of the oldest major religions in the Indian subcontinent —Buddhism. The Buddhist 12th Rock Edict of Emperor Ashoka's reign (268–232 BCE) declares: 'His Sacred Majesty the King does reverence to men of all sects.' After his bloody conquest of Kalinga, Emperor Ashoka became a pacifist and converted to the Buddhist faith. Expectedly, he tried his utmost to spread the Buddhist faith in the subcontinent, and even beyond. Yet, in later centuries, Buddhists and followers of other religious sects in India were either persecuted by some monarchs or co-opted into the Hindu faith, by means of persuasion or coercion. By the tenth century CE, Buddhists and Buddhism had virtually disappeared from the Indian subcontinent.

Here are examples of the whimsical nature of most monarchs. The Hindu king Deva Raya II (1424–1446), of the southern kingdom of Vijayanagara, used to place a copy of the Holy Quran on a stool before him, so that Muslim royal visitors were saved the embarrassment of bowing down to someone they considered to be an infidel ruler. Later Vijayanagara kings were by no means as sensitive to the needs of followers of other religions and did away with the practice. Again, in 1562, the Mughal Emperor Akbar had abolished the hated *jiziya* or religious tax that had been imposed on non-Muslims by earlier rulers. Akbar's descendant, Aurangzeb, whose reign lasted from 1659 to 1707, re-imposed the jiziya tax for a period of time.

There are more egregious instances of policy reversals in the European continent. Given the context of sectarian warfare in Europe in the sixteenth and seventeenth centuries, the Protestant (or 'Huguenot') French king, Henry IV (1553–1610), issued the Edict of Nantes in 1598, granting substantial rights to Huguenots in a predominantly Catholic country, France. All these rights were simply reversed by another French king, Louis XIV (1638–1715), thereby leading to an exodus of Huguenots from France.[8]

From these examples, it is obvious that a theocracy, or a state which establishes one religion,[9] cannot be depended upon to provide lasting toleration to all the different religious groups within the boundaries of the state. In a theocracy, all citizens do not enjoy freedom of religion. At times a theocratic monarch or leader may be benevolent and grant freedoms to 'minority' religions; at other times, he or she may withdraw these freedoms and even begin to persecute those who do not belong to the state's established religion, whether it is Hinduism, Islam or Christianity. If all religious believers—and even non-believers—are to be treated alike, we need a democracy (rule by many) or a republic (rule of law). In short, toleration is a necessary virtue in a polity, but it is not sufficient to establish a lasting secular state.

b) Very clearly, Locke believes that atheists, or non-believers, do not qualify as candidates for freedom of religion within a polity. Locke held the view that all religious believers should be given equal freedom of conscience. The question to be asked is whether Locke is actually pleading for a 'secular state' or merely a 'tolerant state' in *A Letter Concerning Toleration*. According to political theorist Rajeev Bhargava, it would seem to be the latter. Bhargava states: 'A secular state is to be distinguished not only from a theocracy but also from a state where religion is established. It is a state in which religion has been disestablished. The disestablishment of religion means the separation of the state not merely from one but from all religions... A secular state is not anti-religious but exists and survives only when religion is no longer hegemonic. It admits a more general equality between believers and unbelievers.'[10]

There is a crucial difference between a state that establishes one hegemonic religion, while disenfranchising the rest, and a state of 'multiple establishment', which acknowledges and respects all the religions within the polity. The latter is what John Locke is asking for in *A Letter Concerning Toleration*. But Locke's 'multiple establishment' state wants freedom for *all* religions, whereas a secular state wants *both* freedom for all religions *and* freedom from religion itself. This is a crucial difference and means that a secular state gives rights to religious communities as well as to individuals, who may or may not be religious believers.

c) By making it clear that the government should not interfere in citizens' religious beliefs, Locke made a case for the privatization of religious affairs. Indeed, in political terms, Locke is viewed as a great defender of liberalism and a proponent of the Glorious Revolution of 1688–89, which established the primacy of the Parliament over the monarchy, with the dismissal of the Roman Catholic monarch, James II of England (previously, James VII of Scotland), and the installation on the English throne of his Protestant daughter, Mary, and her Protestant Dutch husband, William of Orange.

In *Two Treatises of Government* (1689), Locke points out that man is a creation of God's workmanship, and the philosopher uses this workmanship argument to politically challenge—in the *First Treatise*—Sir Robert Filmer's patriarchal absolutism, by claiming that God created all men as equals, and therefore no man can have dominion over another. Such a move could be classified as the politicization of God by Locke, especially when he calls Him the 'one sovereign master' in the beginning of the *Second Treatise*. By politicizing God, Locke manages to elevate both the moral and political status of men. 'Thus the relation between God and man [in Locke's work] is expressed with reference to a number of different political relationships which variously embody God as king, sole lord, and sovereign master, as well as Maker and Creator. God must be all-powerful, of course, otherwise he is no God.' If man is created in God's own likeness, then he, too, is capable of 'Dominion'.[11]

If we take points a), b), and c) together, we find that John Locke, in the seventeenth century, called for a liberal, multi-establishment state with freedom of religion for all believers (rather than for religious institutions, given his allergy to the Catholic Church as an institution), and a separation of state and religion. This is just a small step away from the non-establishment state called for in the First Amendment to the US Constitution in 1791: 'Congress shall make no law respecting an establishment of religion or prohibiting the free exercise thereof.'

Thomas Jefferson, who was greatly influenced by the ideas of John Locke, had a significant role in drafting the American Constitution and in framing the First Amendment, which enforces the separation between religion and state, forbids the establishment of a national religion, and assures of the right to free exercise of religion. It is interesting to observe here that the phrase, 'wall of separation between church and state' was first coined by Jefferson in his letter of 1802 to the Danbury Baptist Association.

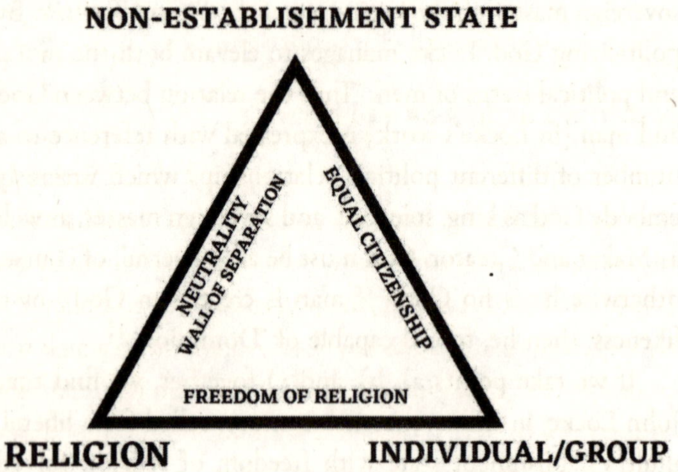

Figure 1

Apart from freedom of religion, a democratic and secular state should guarantee all other freedoms to its citizens. This would require equality of free citizenship. In short, a non-establishment state would guarantee a triple-value form of secularism:

i. Separation of state and religion, which could be taken to mean 'state neutrality', or the harder line of 'wall-of-separation'. The wall of separation between state and religion was formally established as a state policy in France in 1905;
ii. freedom of religion (guaranteed to members of religious groups) and freedom from religion (guaranteed to individuals);

iii. equality of citizenship, guaranteeing all other freedoms to all citizens in a polity.

Secularism in the USA and France

It is important to note that both the United States of America and France have struggled with the establishment of a wall of separation between state and religion. In the United States of America, the wall-of-separation policy was an important corollary to the First Amendment which was passed in 1791 in order to avoid sectarian strife in the country. However, it was not binding on all the states, owing to the country's federal structure.

It was only after the American Civil War (1861–65) that the Fourteenth Amendment was passed in 1868, making the Bill of Rights—as the first ten Amendments to the US constitution are called—applicable to all American states. Despite the passing of the Fourteenth Amendment, some states in the country continued to establish religions and even enact Inquisition-like laws to oppress 'heretics'. In the 1870s, American presidents had to speak out in favour of principles enshrined in the Constitution and reiterate the need to apply secular principles to all the states. But it was not until the 1940s that the United States Supreme Court had occasion to apply the First Amendment's clauses to the states and declare the separation of religion and state as constitutional law. Nevertheless, in the present day, racism and anti-Islamism (after the 11 September 2001

Islamist terrorist attacks in New York and Washington, DC) constitute the biggest threats to America's secular democracy.

In France, soon after the French Revolution of 1789, the monarchy was overthrown, a republic was established, and all ecclesiastical property was at the disposal of the nation. In September 1791, the popular French revolutionary leader, Adrien Duport, urged his colleagues in the Constituent Assembly to decree that French Jews had the same active citizenship rights as those belonging to all Christian sects. This radical move, which had been inspired by the First Amendment of the American Constitution, was reversed by Napoleon Bonaparte, a Corsican soldier, after the fall of the Republicans in 1799.

Napoleon Bonaparte (1769–1821), who became head of the First French Republic in 1799, restored monarchy in France in 1804, by declaring himself Emperor. However, he did manage to institute a Civil Code and effect some remarkable changes in the direction of secular principles. Napoleon ensured that the French state did not establish the Catholic religion. The state paid the salaries of clerics in all the Christian sects and denominations. In 1830, nine years after Napoleon's death, the French state started paying the salaries of Jewish rabbis. In a sense, under Napoleon, the church was in the state, but the state was not in the church. Catholics, Huguenots, Lutherans, Calvinists, Gallicanists, Deists and Jews were all allowed freedom of worship.

After a brief republican interlude between 1848 and 1852, it was only in 1870, in the aftermath of the Franco-Prussian war, that Emperor Napoleon III stepped down and the Third Republic was established. Jules Ferry (1832–1893) was first education minister and then twice Premier of France and was known to be a great promoter of laïcité or secularism. Ferry secularized education and healthcare, by excluding the church from these realms. By 1880, Ferry had also made school education free and compulsory for all children. There was no religious instruction in public schools and children were taught to be republican in thought. No external or visible religious symbol was allowed in state-run educational or healthcare institutions in France.

Secularism, as conceived in the Third Republic, was put to the test in the last decade of the nineteenth century, when there was a court case which had huge repercussions in France. Alfred Dreyfus (1859–1935), a French artillery officer of Jewish background was falsely accused in 1894 of spying for Germany, or Prussia, as it was then known. Even though the real culprit in this treason case was identified in 1896, the French army high command, in cahoots with the Catholic Church, suppressed the news. Owing to the pressure put on the French government by several writers and public intellectuals, Dreyfus was pardoned in 1899, but again put on trial and declared guilty of treason. On 12 July 1906, Dreyfus was formally exonerated by a military commission.

The Dreyfus case had divided France on ideological grounds to such an extent that when the socialists came to power, they immediately passed legislation in 1905 on the wall of separation between religion and the state. The wall of separation ensures that the state does not discriminate against any citizen because of his or her religious affiliation.

More recently, France has faced another kind of turbulence with respect to its secular policies. The most important reason for this is the migration to France in the 1960s from the western part of North Africa, known as the Maghreb, which had been brutally colonized by the French government since 1830. The Maghrebins—Moroccans, Algerians, Tunisians—brought with them the religion of Islam, thereby posing challenges to French laïcité, which had been defined in very narrow terms by Jules Ferry at the end of the nineteenth century. Till the 1960s, there was no sizeable Muslim population in France to disrupt Jules Ferry's conception of secularism for a Judaeo-Christian population. Once the composition of the French population changed in terms of introducing new religions into the mixture, secularism needed to be redefined to emphasize religious freedom rather than the wall of separation between state and religion.

Today, the most important challenge facing French secularism or laïcité is that of having to learn to accommodate the principle of religious pluralism within its polity. The French state seems to favour the wall of separation when it comes to judging the Muslim hijab, the Jewish yarmulke, or the Sikh turban; the same state is more permissive when it concerns the religious freedom of carrying the Christian cross on one's person, if it is hidden from view. In 2011, both France and Belgium banned the wearing of the burqa, or face veil, in public. Canada, Germany, Denmark and Spain have also placed certain restrictions on the wearing of the burqa by Muslim women. Religious freedom for certain religious minority groups is clearly under threat in the West, even though secularism as an ideal is broadly adhered to. When one group of persons is discriminated against in a country on the basis of colour, race, caste or religion, then both democracy and religion are at stake.

The Indian Context

The first official document in the Indian subcontinent which referred to 'equal treatment of all religions'—which is a form of 'state neutrality'—was the Proclamation of Queen Victoria issued in 1858, in the aftermath of the rather violent 1957 Sepoy Revolt. The sepoys in the army, both Hindu and Muslim, revolted fiercely when they discovered the use of beef and pork fat in the greasing of the cartridges, which needed to be bitten before loading them in the new Enfield rifles. It was generally felt that the sentiments of Hindus and Muslims had been offended by the use of animal fat that was considered to be taboo in their religions.

Queen Victoria's Proclamation thus read as follows:

'We declare it to be our royal will and pleasure that none be in anywise favoured, none molested or disquieted, by reason of their religious faith or observances, but that all alike shall enjoy the equal and impartial protection of the law; and we do strictly charge and enjoin all those who may be in authority under us that they abstain from all interference with the religious belief or worship of any of our subjects on pain of our highest displeasure.' This section of the Proclamation inaugurated a new British colonial policy of support for non-interference in matters of religious belief or worship within British India.

Of course, nearly a century earlier, there had been the Warren Hastings Regulating Plan of 1772, which had established a judicial system that codified civil, commercial and criminal laws. Family and inheritance laws were as yet in the private domain and governed by myriad Hindu and Muslim personal codes. No doubt, by 1882, all laws—with the exception of personal laws—were governed by the British colonial administration. After Independence in 1947, the Indian Parliament modified and revised Hindu personal laws in 1955–56, by abolishing polygamy and permitting divorce. Although these changes concerned the Hindu Code, non-Hindu groups like Buddhists, Jains and Sikhs were brought under its purview. Interestingly enough, during the Constituent Assembly Debates, these three non-Hindu groups—Buddhists, Jains and Sikhs—had demanded their own personal codes, but these were denied to them.

India is presently home to eight major religions of the world: Hinduism, Sikhism, Buddhism, Jainism, Islam, Christianity, Zoroastrianism and Judaism. Non-establishment was a necessary part of Indian secularism, to assure religious minorities of their equal participation in the new Indian republic. It was also important to show the world that India was not like Pakistan—a country which was founded and established as a Muslim state.

The strength of a secular state lies in the way it treats its minorities, whether they are religious minorities or lower-caste minorities. Here, it is important to qualify the term 'minority', which is not necessarily a numerical concept. A minority, especially in the Indian context, has a low level of status and power in the present time. Muslims and Christians may have flourished in earlier times; today, both religions are under siege, and Muslims have very low representation in the army, the police force or the civil services.

In the early part of the twentieth century, the Morley–Minto Reforms of 1909 had provided for reserved seats for Muslims in legislatures in India through a system of separate electorates. This British colonial legislation was viewed by some Indian nationalists as a part of the 'divide-and-rule' policy of the colonial power and bitterly resented. In fact, the extreme reaction to counter the effects of this policy was the founding of the Hindu Mahasabha in 1915 by Lala Lajpat Rai and Madan Mohan Malaviya. During the Constituent Assembly Debates, it was clear that the demand for separate electorates for Muslims would not be entertained at all, though seats were sought to be reserved under a different system (see Chapter II).

Lower castes—i.e. Dalits, Adivasis, and the Most Backward Classes (MBCs) among the Other Backward Classes (OBCs)—may be a numerically large group. However, they continue to face tremendous social discrimination at the hands of the upper-caste groups. This is why equality of opportunity is simply not enough to address the issue of social discrimination.

Even in the late 1940s, during the Constituent Assembly Debates, it was recognized that formal equality or equality of opportunity would not be adequate to address historical disadvantages suffered by the lower castes. Therefore, in the Indian Constitution, there is provision for special treatment, including reservation in services, education and legislatures, for Scheduled Castes and Scheduled Tribes. The Constitution has made provision for both individual and community rights. In other words, equality of citizenship includes—in the case of some communities—the notion of differential citizenship. Such special treatment to disadvantaged groups enhances the democratic principle of equality, because it aims to bring about a more equal distribution of education, employment and representation for different sections of the population, who have differential disadvantages at birth.

Here are the relevant Constitutional provisions:

> Article 15(4): Nothing in this article or in clause (2) of article 29[12] shall prevent the state from making any special provision for the advancement of any socially and educationally backward classes of citizens or for the Scheduled Castes and the Scheduled Tribes.
>
> Article 16(4): Nothing in this article shall prevent the state from making any provision for the reservation of appointments or posts in favour of any backward class of citizens which, in the opinion of the state, is not adequately represented in the services under the state.
>
> Article 330(1): Seats shall be reserved in the House of the People for—
>
> a) The Scheduled Castes;
> b) The Scheduled Tribes
>
> Article 332(1): Seats shall be reserved for the Scheduled Castes and the Scheduled Tribes...in the Legislative Assembly of every state.

Let us also look at some important constitutional amendments with respect to reservations. For example, the 73rd Constitutional Amendment Act, 1992, which stipulated the following:

- In every Gram Panchayat, seats must be set aside for members of Scheduled Castes and Scheduled Tribes. The percentage of these seats to the total number of seats in the Panchayat that are to be filled through direct elections must be as close to equal as possible.

- Women from Scheduled Castes or, where applicable, Scheduled Tribes must have access to at least one-third of the seats that are set aside for them.
- Not less than one-third (including the number of seats reserved for women belonging to the Scheduled Castes and the Scheduled Tribes) of the total number of seats to be filled by direct elections in every Gram Panchayat shall be reserved for women and such seats may be allotted by rotation to different constituencies in a Gram Panchayat in such manner as may be prescribed.
- The above reservation was provided for the position of chairpersons of the panchayat too. The Act also authorizes the legislature of the state to make reservations for backward classes.

There was also the 74th Constitutional Amendment Act, 1992, brought in to ensure adequate representation of Scheduled Castes and Scheduled Tribes and of women in the municipal bodies also. It stated: 'The proportion of seats to be reserved for SC/ST to the total number of seats shall be same as the proportion of the population of SC/ST in the municipal area. The reservation would be made in respect of seats to be filled by direct elections only. Not less than one-third of the total number of seats reserved for SC/ST shall be reserved for women belonging to SC/ST. This is a mandatory provision. In respect of women, the seats shall be reserved to the extent of not less than one-third of the total number of seats. This includes seats reserved for women belonging to SC/ST. These reservations will apply for direct elections only. This is also a mandatory provision. There will be no bar on State Legislatures from making provisions for reservation of seats in any municipality or office of Chairperson in the municipalities in favour of backward class of citizens. This is an optional provision.'

Those who believe that equality of opportunity should suffice for the cause of democracy are grossly mistaken. Advanced countries like Canada and Australia have instituted special cultural rights, special representation and rights to autonomy for traditionally disadvantaged groups like the Inuit, the Native Americans and the Aborigines. These rights, known as multicultural rights, are really a product of the 1990s onwards. In this sense, some of the provisions of the 1949 Indian Constitution are far beyond their time and may be viewed as multicultural or special safeguards for vulnerable groups. Articles 15(4), 16(4), 330(1), 332(1), 370, 29 and 30 are some of the most progressive provisions in the Constitution. These provisions go beyond secular principles, like freedom of religion and equal citizenship, and perhaps even strengthen the concept of secularism by protecting minorities.

Secularism in India—Some Concepts

As we have seen, secularism in the West has often been defined as the separation of state and religion. Against

Locke and Holyoake, Rajeev Bhargava states that 'mere separation of state and religion does not constitute a secular state'.[13] At the same time, secularism is not synonymous with science, rationality, agnosticism, or atheism: '[A] secular state neither mindlessly excludes all religions nor is blindly neutral towards them... A state interfering in one religion more than in others does not automatically depart from secularism. Secularism requires principled distance, not exclusion or equidistance.'[14] Indeed, Bhargava's notion of 'principled distance' refers to the Indian state's action to either aid or regulate the affairs of religions on a principled basis, by taking into consideration the context of each case that needs the state's intervention.

Religious freedom was given to everyone, even though there were initially objections in the Constituent Assembly to the idea of allowing proselytization or religious conversion, especially to religious practitioners of Islam and Christianity. Article 25 of the Indian Constitution (see Chapter II) allows religious practitioners to propagate and convert others to their faith. During the Constituent Assembly Debates, one member put forward the view that propagation of a religion meant freedom of expression, and not freedom to convert others to one's religion, particularly on a mass basis.[15] Another member, Lokanath Misra, did not want religious conversion to be a justiciable right. To this, Rohini Kumar Chaudhury remarked that he had no objection to religious propagation, as long as religious propagandists of one religion did not malign the practices of other religions. T.T. Krishnamachari's perspective was that propagation was part of the practice of almost all religions—whether it was Hinduism, the Arya Samaj, Christianity, Islam, Jainism or Buddhism. And K.M. Munshi added, 'So long as religion is religion, conversion by free exercise of the conscience has to be recognized.'[16]

As much as a year earlier, the member from Bihar, Hussain Imam, had pointed out, in response to Clause 17 of the Report of the Sub-Committee on Fundamental Rights,[17] that 'Forcible conversion is the highest degree of undesirable thing. But it is not proper, as...Sardar [Patel] himself has admitted, to provide it in the justiciable fundamental rights. The only place which it can occupy is in the annals of High Court judgements'.[18] Clause 17 stated: 'Conversion from one religion to another brought about by coercion or undue influence shall not be recognized by law.' Finally, Clause 17 was removed, and it was decided not to attempt to define the scope of religious propagation in the Constitution, but to leave that to the legislatures and law courts, should the need arise in the future (see Chapter III).

There have been other safeguards for the right to freedom of religion, especially in the context of election speeches and rallies. In fact, section 123(2A) of the Representation of the People Act, 1951 states that a corrupt electoral practitioner who 'threatens any candidate or any elector...with injury of any kind, including social ostracism and ex-communication or expulsion from any caste or community', or, again, 'induces or attempts to induce a candidate or an elector to believe that he, or any person in whom he is interested, will become or will be rendered an object of divine displeasure or spiritual censure' is liable to be disqualified in the electoral process or face punitive charges. Section 123(3A) refers to further punitive action against the 'promotion of, or attempt to promote, feelings of enmity or hatred between different classes of the citizens of India on grounds of religion, race, caste, community, or language, by a candidate or his election agent...for the furtherance of the prospects of the election of that candidate or for prejudicially affecting the election of any candidate'. Section 295 in the Indian Penal Code refers to stringent punishment of up to two years with fine for 'injuring or defiling place of worship with intent to insult the religion of any class'.

All these different legal provisions are expected to uphold equal citizenship and freedom of religion in situations that arise in the context of religious conversions, which are anyway allowed by Article 25, as noted above. At the same time, all Indian citizens have a duty as embodied in the Constitution's Article 51A(e) 'to promote harmony and the spirit of common brotherhood among all the people of India transcending religious, linguistic and regional or sectional diversities'.

While the Indian Constitution protects the right to propagate religion, a new discourse has been created to bring in notions of 'inducements' and 'fraud' pertaining to religious conversions. As a contributor to a Western journal has noted: 'The many bills for "religious freedom" in their *very* nomenclature, indicate that they are designed to guard against encroachments upon independent, "indigenous" religious sensibilities and affiliations and are not designed to protect those whose religious viewpoints call for active proselytization. This points to a common bias among many Hindu political leaders and their supporters alike that conversion is a kind of violence or disruption of religious freedoms against which governments should protect their vulnerable citizenries.'[19]

Thus, in many Indian states, the anti-conversion argument has prevailed, and these states have passed the curiously-worded 'Freedom of Religion' Act. Initially, the Freedom of Religion Act was directed at the so-called coercive forms of mass conversion of Scheduled Castes and Scheduled Tribes by Christian missionaries, and states like Madhya Pradesh and Odisha were the first to pass such legislation in the 1960s in independent India. Arunachal Pradesh passed the legislation in 1978, Gujarat and Chhattisgarh in 2003, while Rajasthan and Himachal Pradesh passed similar legislation in 2006. More recently, states like Uttar Pradesh and Karnataka have used and extended the ambit of the Act to direct their ire at the Muslim community. Even state government officials employ terms like 'jihad' or 'militant campaign' to focus on the imagined misdemeanours of

Muslims. For example, when cows are slaughtered[20] by Muslim butchers for local consumption or export of beef, it is dubbed 'beef jihad', and when Muslim youths befriend Hindu girls, it is called 'love jihad'. The suggestion here, with this kind of terminology, is that no activity of Muslims can be trusted. Since the 1980s, the Bharatiya Janata Party, which was formerly constituted as the Jana Sangh, has made a distinction between so-called 'positive secularism', which is rule by Hindu majoritarianism, and 'pseudo-secularism', which, in their opinion, is appeasement of religious minority communities to the detriment of majority Hindu interests.

While the principles of a non-establishment state and freedom of religious practice were included in the Constitution, the separation of state and religion was not, for cultural and pragmatic reasons. Speaking in Parliament on the Hindu Code Bill in 1951, Dr B.R. Ambedkar, Chairman of the Drafting Committee of the Constitution, explained the idea of a non-establishment state as follows: '[The secular state] does not mean that we shall not take into consideration the religious sentiments of the people. All that a secular state means is that this Parliament shall not be competent to impose any particular religion upon the rest of the people.'[21] The right to freedom of religion—Article 25(1) in the Indian Constitution—was discussed in the Fundamental Rights Sub-Committee of the Constituent Assembly in April 1947. The point of contention was the definition of freedom of religion—would it be specified as 'freedom to worship' or 'freedom to practise religion'?

Why was this a controversy, and why did this dichotomous definition of freedom of religion create divisions within the Constituent Assembly?

Those members who opposed the granting of freedom to practise religion, like Rajkumari Amrit Kaur, argued that religious practice in India militated against the interests of women and the lower castes, like the practice of child marriages, dedication of girls to temples, denial of temple entry to lower castes, the obligatory dowry to be given to the groom's family, the purdah system, polygamy, not allowing divorce or reproductive rights to women, and so on. She also did not want religious minorities to set up their own educational institutions or get state funding or aid for them. In fact, in a meeting of the Minorities Sub-Committee in April 1947, Govind Ballabh Pant had wanted cultural and educational rights of minorities (presently, Articles 29 and 30) to be included in the Directive Principles section, as non-justiciable rights, in the Constitution.

Those who argued in favour of granting freedom of religious practice endorsed cultural, educational and political safeguards for minority groups, as well as retaining the personal law codes for different religious communities. Among others in the Constituent Assembly, Maulana Hasrat Mohani made an impassioned plea in favour of retaining personal law codes for the religious minorities: 'I would like to say that any party, political or communal, has no right to interfere in the personal law of any group.'[22] Another member, Mahboob Ali Baig Sahib Bahadur lamented that there was nowhere in the Constitution any mention of provisions safeguarding the personal law of minorities.[23] But another Muslim member, Tajamul Hussain, argued that 'this is a secular state, and a secular state should not have anything to do with religion. So I would request you to leave me alone, to practise and profess my own religion privately'.[24]

Given the public nature of worship and practice—both of which were finally guaranteed by the Constitution—of most religions in India, it would have been very difficult to relegate religion to the private sphere. Furthermore, nearly all religions depended on the state for support and active intervention to safeguard their activities. Gurpreet Mahajan explains this phenomenon as being peculiar to the subcontinent: 'If religious practice entails that members of a community have the liberty to immerse the idol of Durga in running water, or to gather for a holy dip in Ganga on the day of full Kumbh or at Allahabad on the last day of the month of "Shravana", the state would have to accommodate that. It would have to make arrangements to facilitate the observance of these practices. The right to religious practice thus gave religion and religious groups an opportunity to be highly visible in the public arena, to carry processions outside of their designated place of worship, and to stamp their presence in the public domain.'[25] All the same, as various Indian court judgements reveal, the tension between religious freedom and state interference has persisted to the present day.

In sum, the Indian Constitution guaranteed secularism as follows:

i. Rejection of a theocratic state and adoption of a non-establishment state;
ii. acceptance of religion as both an individual right and a group right;
iii. interference of the state in religious affairs on a principled (or case-to-case) basis; and
iv. equality of citizenship, under which is subsumed the idea of differential citizenship for specific, disadvantaged communities.

In fact, in India, this is what the 'secular triangle' would look like:

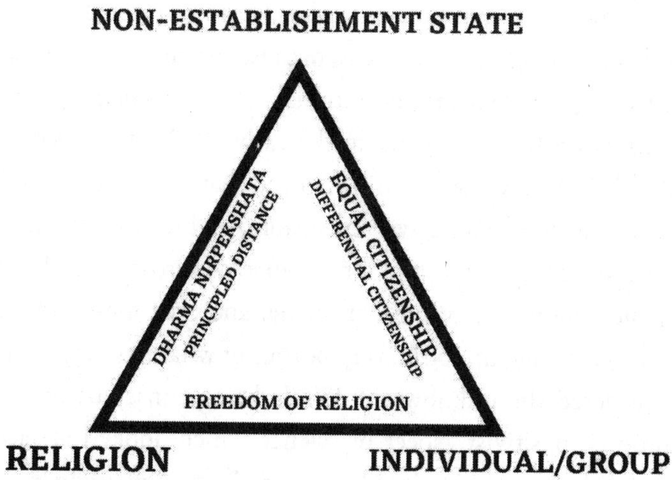

Figure 2

Secularism and Indian Nationalists

How did Indian nationalists look at the idea of a secular state in post-Independence India? The views on secularism and religion of India's first prime minister, Jawaharlal Nehru, are fairly well known, considering his own role in the formulation of the new Hindu Code in the mid-1950s. Between 1955 and 1958, Nehru passed the Hindu Marriage Act, Hindu Succession Act, Hindu Minority and Guardianship Act, and the Hindu Adoptions and Maintenance Act. Nehru studied natural sciences at Trinity College, Cambridge, and espoused the need for 'a scientific temper' and rationality at a time when most Indians, especially in rural areas, were in the grip of superstition and illiteracy.

One of the main reasons why Nehru did not consider himself a religious man was because of his unequivocal reverence for scientific and rational values. In *The Discovery of India* (written in prison in the early 1940s, published in 1946), Nehru wrote: 'I am convinced that the methods and approach of science have revolutionized human life more than anything else in the long course of history, and have opened doors and avenues of further and even more radical change, leading up to the very portals of what has long been considered the unknown.'[26] While being conscious of the limiting, positivist aspect of science which 'looked at fact alone', Nehru also pointed out that '[r]eligion, though it has undoubtedly brought comfort to innumerable human beings and stabilized society by its values, has checked the tendency to change and progress inherent in human society... Realizing [the] limitations of reason and scientific method, we have still to hold on to them with all our strength, for without that firm basis and background we can have no grip on any kind of truth or reality'.[27]

Nehru wanted a liberal, secular state that would focus on individual rights. As a consequence, he strongly objected to public functionaries attending religious events. When President Rajendra Prasad attended the inauguration of the Somnath Temple in Gujarat, Nehru censured Prasad's act as a travesty of the principle of separation between state and religion. In reality, the Indian Constitution did not—or could not—endorse this principle, and permitted state intervention in religious matters, albeit on a 'principled' basis. Unsurprisingly, the doyen of Indian philosophy and second President of India, Sarvepalli Radhakrishnan, held the opinion that 'the religious impartiality of the Indian State is not to be confused with secularism or atheism. Secularism as here defined is in accordance with the ancient religious tradition of India.'[28] In his famous 1926 Upton Lectures, Radhakrishnan had, for the first time, referred to Hinduism as 'a way of life', thereby distinguishing it from other major religions in India. This description of Hinduism would have repercussions seven decades later, in the mid-1990s, in what would be known as the 'Hindutva judgements' (see Chapter III).

During the Constituent Assembly Debates, Govind Malaviya wanted a reference to the 'Supreme Power which guides the destinies of the whole world' in the Preamble to the Constitution, on the ground that more than 90 per cent of Indians were staunch religious believers.[29] On the other hand, K.T. Shah wanted a new article inserted to the effect: 'The State in India being secular shall have no concern with any religion, creed or profession of faith; and shall observe an attitude of absolute neutrality in all matters relating to the religion of any class of its citizens or other persons in the Union.'[30] While K.T. Shah tried to incorporate the sentence, 'India shall be a Secular, Federal, Socialist Union of States' in clause (1) of Article 1, H.V. Kamath was of the opinion that the words 'secular' and 'socialist' should only appear in the Preamble.[31]

Of course, none of these proposed amendments were taken on board by the Drafting Committee. One analyst put it this way: 'On the one hand, religious and cultural diversities made secularism indispensable for democracy and national integration. On the other was the impending task of modernizing our traditional society and bringing in social reform that required state intervention in religious affairs... Given the polemic over the inclusion of the term, it was not included in the 1950 Constitution.'[32] Kamath's suggestion that the word 'secular' should appear in the Preamble was fulfilled finally by the 42nd Constitutional Amendment in September 1976—bang in the middle of

Indira Gandhi's Emergency! This amendment enjoined all citizens to consider it their fundamental duty to 'preserve the rich heritage of our composite culture'.[33]

Soon after Independence in August 1947, Nehru started writing letters on every possible subject to chief ministers, and this process went on till December 1963, that is to say, a few months before his death in 1964. These letters were published, some 20 years later, in the form of five thick volumes. Among these were quite a few letters pertaining to India's religious minorities, especially the Indian Muslim community, which had become one of the most vulnerable groups within the Indian polity, particularly in the bloody aftermath of Partition of the subcontinent in August 1947.

In a letter dated 15 October 1947, Nehru ridiculed the prevailing notion among certain sections of Hindu society that the central government was following a 'policy of appeasement' as far as the Muslim community was concerned. Showing considerable prescience, he wrote: 'We have a Muslim minority who are so large in numbers that they cannot, even if they want to, go somewhere else. They have got to live in India. That is a basic fact about which there can be no argument. Whatever the provocation from Pakistan and whatever the indignities and horrors inflicted on non-Muslims there, we have got to deal with the minority in a civilized manner. We must give them security and the rights of citizens in a democratic State. If we fail to do so, we shall have a festering sore which will eventually poison the whole body politic and probably destroy it.'

Many analysts of the nationalist movement, especially of events in the 1920s, 1930s and 1940s, commonly referred to M.K. Gandhi's religiosity and Jawaharlal Nehru's secularism in antagonistic terms. Contemporary writers tend to project nationalists like Gandhi and Nehru from a somewhat narrow or partial perspective. For example, those who believe that Gandhi was not a secularist selectively quote from his writings the following sentence: 'Those who say religion has nothing to do with politics do not know what religion is.' Rather than interpreting this sentiment as evidence of Gandhi's opposition to secularism, we could say that he merely attempted 'to make religion more tolerant and politics more moral'.[34] Gandhi is variously viewed as a pre-modern anti-secularist, or as a traditionalist who subverts the liberal project, or again, as a prototype of the contemporary divisive communalist. As a well-known analyst points out, 'Such a [partial] reading denies us the advantage of the richer, more enabling legacy which I feel is of continuing relevance to us today.'[35]

For example, while Gandhi wrote in *Young India* on 2 March 1922 that 'human mind or human society is not divided into watertight compartments called social, political and religious', he modified his ideas on the same subject in *Harijan* on 29 June 1947: 'Religion is no test of nationality, but a personal matter between man and God. In the sense of nationality they are Indians first and Indians last, no matter what religion they profess.'

In 1930, Gandhi had used the phrase, '*sarva dharma sambhaav*', to indicate that all religions are equally worthy of respect. With this phrase, Gandhi did not necessarily imply some sort of state neutrality and that the state should treat all religions with equal respect, because he genuinely felt that the state had no business at all in religious affairs.[36] One explanation given is that, for Gandhi, 'a secularized world is essentially unstable, because it elevates everything to the level of instrumental rationality'.[37]

Not all analysts hold the view that Gandhi was wary of the idea of secularism. According to Thomas Pantham, Gandhi believed that every religion contained the following ethical elements—an ethics of toleration, an ethics of truth or *satya*, and an ethics of non-violence or *ahimsa*. As Pantham puts it: 'Gandhi pioneered a way of moral-political experimentation in which the relative autonomy (or non-absolute separation) of religion and politics from each other is used for the reconstruction of both the religious traditions and the modern state.'[38] Later on, one more phrase was added to the lexicon of Indian secularism, namely '*dharma nirpekshata*' or state neutrality.

Malabika Pande[39] goes even further in order to firmly establish Gandhi's role as a secularist. Pande suggests that Gandhi's frequent use of the term '*ramarajya*' ('Kingdom of the god Ram') was 'really a synonym for ethical rules based on the consent of the governed where public opinion was highly valued'.[40] In fact, according to Pande, Gandhi endorsed all three values of secularism—freedom of religion for all, equal citizenship and separation of religion and state.

Gandhi emphasized the importance of mutual toleration in a pluralist society such as ours, thereby ensuring freedom of religion for everyone. Gandhi's vision of citizenship included civic rights and duties of all citizens, and the right to dissent in the face of political, social and economic deprivation. Gandhi's own agitations and protests—the Rowlatt satyagraha, the Jallianwala Bagh protest, the Vaikom satyagraha, the Khilafat agitation—are illustrative of his vision in this regard. Regarding Gandhi's participation in the Khilafat agitation (for which he was severely criticized by many writers), Pande says: 'One may criticize Gandhi's choice of a strictly religious issue for a national campaign in a multi-religious country, but no one can doubt his secular motivation and his objective of promoting the emotional integration of the country.'[41]

Gandhi's anti-caste agitations were initially planned during the All-India Social Conference at Calcutta, December 1917. Subsequently, Gandhi pressed for the education of the Depressed Classes, emphasized the need to respect dignity of labour, and enforced the notion of equality of treatment for these Classes in all institutions. In the broader area of education, Gandhi established the first national university in Ahmedabad, the 'Gujarat Vidyapith', in 1921. He strongly condemned 'communal' institutions like the Aligarh Muslim University, Khalsa College, Amritsar and the Benares Hindu University.[42]

As far as the third secular value, the relationship between state and religion, was concerned, Gandhi believed that the state, having no business in religion, should neither support nor aid any religion or religious group. He thought of enabling an autonomous body, a Board of Arbitration, to mediate inter-communal dialogue, disputes or conflicts.

In conclusion, Pande states, 'Gandhi's secularism did indeed represent an inclusive approach which denoted an equal regard for all faiths. But he was clear that faiths, like culture, had to evolve... A multi-cultural nation would always have to adopt a strong secular policy if it desired to retain its virility.'[43]

Despite the fact that Gandhi understood the value of secularism in the new Indian nation-state, he did not participate in the Constituent Assembly Debates (1946–49). However, his long shadow did influence, in various ways, the proceedings within the Assembly, especially those connected to discussions on secularism.

Chapter II

Debating Secularism

Some of the most fascinating debates in India on the subject of secularism have been the Constituent Assembly Debates (CAD) from December 1946 to November 1949.[44] Reading the debates on matters pertaining to secularism is like witnessing a theatrical production, the script of which continues to unravel even in the present day.

However, before we start discussing the Debates, we need to ask the question: why do we need a Constitution? The obvious answer is that a Constitution can check the unbridled power of—and abuse by—the state. It can also lead to radical social transformation by peaceful and democratic means. Finally, we need the Constitution to protect individuals and minority groups in the polity against majoritarian fallibility. Dr B.R. Ambedkar, the Chairman of the Drafting Committee, believed that a good and effective constitution could herald an era of liberty, equality and fraternity.

Some earlier drafts of the Indian Constitution had appeared decades before the 1940s. The trigger for Indians wanting to get their own constitution was the appointment of an all-white British committee known as the 'Simon Commission' in November 1927, which was expected to review the working of the 1909 Government of India Act. In the following month, in its Madras session, the Indian National Congress decided to boycott the Simon Commission and fashion its own constitution, through a committee chaired by Motilal Nehru, to look into the problem of religious communalism in the subcontinent, and at the possibility of Dominion Status for the country. The Motilal Nehru Report, comprising 22 chapters and 87 articles, was submitted at the All Parties Conference in August 1929. Because this draft constitution rejected 'separate electorates' for Muslims, but recommended social and cultural rights for religious minorities, it was not accepted by the Muslim League under the leadership of M.A. Jinnah. The Indian Councils Act of 1909, also known as the Morley–Minto Reforms, had introduced separate electorates on the basis of religion, and the Muslim community was a major beneficiary of this piece of colonial legislation.

Interestingly, Articles XI, XII, XIII of the Motilal Nehru Report read as follows:

XI. 'There shall be no state religion for the Commonwealth of India or for any province in the

Commonwealth, nor shall the state either directly or indirectly endow any religion or give any preference or impose any disability on account of religious belief or religious status.'

XII. 'No person attending any school receiving state aid or other public money shall be compelled to attend the religious instruction that may be given in the school.'

XIII. 'No person shall, by reason of his religion, caste or creed be prejudiced in any way in regard to public employment, office of power or honour and the exercise of any trade or calling.'

Elaborating on the conclusions of the 1928 Motilal Nehru Report, Neera Chandhoke says: 'In sum...the rights of minority communities to their religion and culture were recognized partly to allay the fears of the religious minorities, party to neutralize the demand for separate electorates by the Muslims, and partly to devise a principle that could regulate inter-group relationships within the Congress coalition... Group rights were granted to create the conditions for a mass struggle as well as to offset the fears of the religious minorities that they would be swamped in a majoritarian India. Therefore, in 1928, the Motilal Nehru Constitution granted to *all* religious communities the right to their language, script, culture, and religious practices.'[45]

Jawaharlal Nehru and other Congress leaders had also opposed the Government of India Act of 1935 as an imposition on Indians by the British colonial government. This Act comprised provisions for administration and governance by the British colonial government, but also introduced the bicameral legislative system, which was later adopted by the Indian Constituent Assembly in the form of the two Houses of Parliament, Lok Sabha (as well as Legislative Assemblies in the states) and Rajya Sabha (including Legislative Councils in the states).

Following the failure of the Gandhi–Jinnah talks in 1944 to prevent Partition of the subcontinent, the Constitutional Proposals of the Sapru Committee, also known as the Sapru Committee Report, was published in 1945. Well-known lawyer Tej Bahadur Sapru headed this thirty-member Committee, whose brief was 'to examine the whole communal and minorities question from a constitutional and political point of view, put itself in touch with the different parties and their leaders, including the minorities interested in the question, and present a solution'. Rejecting the Muslim League's demand for Pakistan, the Report called for all kinds of fundamental freedoms for all Indian citizens, including religious freedom and equality. It recommended that the constitution-making body should have equal representation of Hindus and Muslims, and that 'Muslim representation...shall be on a par with the representation given to the Hindus (other than Scheduled Castes)' in the Union legislature on the basis of joint electorates. The representation of the minority communities in the executive was expected to be a reflection of the Union legislature. In the fundamental rights section, there were provisions for full religious toleration, including non-interference in religious beliefs, practices and institutions, and protection of languages and cultures of all communities. Each of the provinces would have an independent minority commission, whose members would oversee the interests of minority communities in the area.

The creation of a brand-new constitution in India was therefore an occasion for tremendous anticipation and excitement. The Constituent Assembly had seven of the thirty members from the Sapru Committee. In early 1947, B.N. Rau, the Constitutional Advisor to the Assembly, had circulated a questionnaire concerning the provision to be made for the adequate representation of all communities in the central and provincial legislatures. As Shefali Jha points out: 'Hardly anyone replied to this questionnaire',[46] except for S.P. Mukherjee and K.M. Panikkar, both of whom recommended proportional representation for Muslims, Sikhs, Anglo-Indians, Indian Christians, Scheduled Castes, particularly in the Upper House, the Rajya Sabha.

The duration of the Constituent Assembly Debates was marked by several demands by minority groups, comprising religious minorities, Scheduled Castes, and Scheduled Tribes. These demands were for reservation in legislatures and the services, for separate electorates, and for proportional representation, and they were made with a view to attenuating the ill-effects of a Hindu-majority government, which could easily ride roughshod over the legitimate views and aspirations of different minority groups in the polity. These views and aspirations are of crucial importance in a discussion on Indian secular democracy because they pertain to one wing of the 'secular triangle', namely, Citizenship. The question here is: How do the Indian state and society see its citizens—as equal, or unequal, depending on their caste and community affiliation? The answer to this question will have profound consequences for our secular democracy.

Let us therefore try to understand the terms 'separate electorates' and 'proportional representation' before we proceed any further.

Some Definitions

The system of separate electorates implies that members of a particular community or group may choose their leader (or leaders) for a reserved seat (or seats) in a separate election in constituencies that are earmarked for them. As mentioned above, the first award of separate electorates was introduced for Muslims in the first Councils Act (also known as the Morley–Minto reforms) of 1909. This award was extended to Sikhs, Indian Christians, Anglo-Indians and Europeans by the Government of India Act, 1919. Indeed, the first demand for separate electorates by the Scheduled Castes was made after the Round Table Conferences (1930–32), when the British prime minister, Ramsay MacDonald, accorded seventy-two seats out of a total of approximately 1,580 seats—on the basis of separate electorates—to the Scheduled Castes (also known as 'untouchables' or 'Harijans' or 'Dalits').

Since Mohandas Karamchand Gandhi firmly believed that Scheduled Castes were part of the larger Hindu community, he opposed their award of a separate electorate, and went on an indefinite fast as a method of moral persuasion for those who opposed him. Finally, Dr B.R. Ambedkar, the influential leader of Scheduled Castes, knuckled under the moral pressure put on the community by Gandhi, and came to an agreement in the Poona Pact, which effectively did away with the communal award of a separate electorate, and gave 151 seats to Scheduled Castes in a system of caste-based reservation under a joint electorate. A joint electorate implies a system of adult franchise where all adult citizens are eligible to vote. While Dr Ambedkar thought that it was important for the Scheduled Castes to choose their own leaders, Gandhi believed in a system of caste-based reservations whereby all voters could choose the Scheduled Caste leaders they wanted in government.

During the Constituent Assembly debates in the late 1940s, when some Muslim members of the Constituent Assembly asked for the revival of separate electorates for their community, Govind Ballabh Pant asked, with a considerable measure of pragmatism: '[W]hat is your ultimate ideal? Do you want a real national secular State or a theocratic State? If the latter, then in this Union of India, a theocratic State can only be a Hindu State.'[47] If there are separate electorates for the minorities, Pant pointed out, the inevitable result would be that the majority would become isolated from the minorities and would not hesitate to harass or persecute the latter. The logic here would have seemed a bit puzzling to the Muslim members posing the question in the Assembly. On the one hand, Pant seemed to suggest that a demand by minority groups for separate electorates was both anti-modern and anti-national, since these groups tacitly wanted a theocratic, not a secular, state. On the other, should the minorities persist with their demand, Pant anticipated a violent reaction from the majority community, which would, in its turn, become anti-modern and would establish a Hindu Rashtra. Ergo, if there was a Hindu Rashtra in the making, it was the fault of the minority communities' incessant demand for greater representation in the polity, which was primarily undertaken to thwart the menace of Hindu upper- and dominant-caste majoritarianism!

Be that as it may, where exactly did the problem lie with joint electorates, as far as the Scheduled Castes and religious minorities were concerned? In a separate electorate system, a Scheduled Caste candidate is chosen by the Scheduled Caste community; in a joint electorate system, the Scheduled Caste candidate is chosen by the political party, comprising *all* castes and communities.

S. Nagappa pointed out in the Constituent Assembly that if no member of the Scheduled Caste community casts a vote for a Scheduled Caste candidate, what credibility would the latter have?[48] Furthermore, how can such a candidate claim to represent his or her community? While S. Nagappa put forth the view that the Scheduled Caste candidate, who is to be elected in a reserved seat in the legislature, should secure at least 35 per cent of the votes from the Scheduled Caste community, K.T.M. Ahmed Ibrahim Sahib Bahadur claimed that the Muslim candidate in a reserved seat should secure at least 30 per cent of the votes from the Muslim community. Of course, the rest of the votes, in both cases, would come from the joint electorate system.[49] In other words, both Nagappa and Ibrahim Sahib were ready to accept a mixed electorate system.

The youngest Scheduled Caste member of the Assembly, Dakshayani Velayudhan, had a different view altogether. Reacting to S. Nagappa's demand for mixed electorates, she said: 'As long as the Scheduled Castes, or the Harijans, or by whatever name they may be called, are economic slaves of other people, there is no meaning demanding either separate electorates or joint electorates... Personally speaking, I am not in favour of any kind of reservation in any place whatsoever.'

Not surprisingly, candidates from the Muslim and the Scheduled Caste communities, who harboured notions of separate electorates, were severely chastised by Sardar

Vallabhbhai Patel: 'If the process that was adopted, which resulted in the separation of the country, is to be repeated, then I say: Those who want that kind of thing have a place in Pakistan, not here (*Applause*)... To the Scheduled Caste friends, I also appeal: Let us forget what you did. You have very nearly escaped partition of the country again on your lines... I feel that the vast majority of the Hindu population wishes you well. Without them where will you be? Therefore, secure their confidence and forget that you are a Scheduled Caste.'[50]

Blaming the British colonialists for the present mess, M. Ananthasayanam Ayyangar pointed out that different communities lived together in harmony in earlier times. Even in the present day, '[u]nder the joint electorate system, a Hindu can represent the Muslims and a Muslim the Hindus'.[51] The fact that separate electorates had been awarded to different categories of the populace by the colonial British government, which consistently followed a 'divide-and-rule' policy, was not forgotten by Indian nationalists. Even if there might have been merit in the arguments in favour of separate electorates, nationalists like Sardar Patel were firmly against the idea on the ground that it would isolate the minorities from mainstream politics. Furthermore, it was believed that separate electorates would create a culture of advocacy rather than authorship of law and policy in the legislatures. By the end of 1947, the demand for separate electorates was more or less given up.

Not all members of religious minority groups endorsed the principle of separate electorates. Z.H. Lari explained why every citizen had a right to representation, while the party with most seats in the legislatures had a right to govern. If the electoral system should ensure representation to everybody, including members of minority groups, then it should adopt the principle of proportional representation. D.H. Chandrasekharaiya, Sardar Hukam Singh, K.T. Shah, and Kazi Syed Karimuddin also demanded proportional representation, although they varied on the mode to be adopted.

Sardar Patel was initially sympathetic to the demand of proportional representation by the minorities. Under this system, parties representing minority group interests would also find a place in the legislatures, because of better and fairer proportionality between the votes and the seats in the legislatures that a political party gets. Proportional representation assumes three main modes or forms: the party-list system, the single transferable vote and cumulative voting. In the first-past-the-post system, the candidate who gets more votes than any other is deemed to have won. If only two candidates are contesting, the winning candidate needs to get at least 51 per cent of the total number of votes cast. If three or more candidates are contesting, the winning candidate could get a small percentage of the total votes cast, but his or her share will be higher than that obtained by any other contestant. In other words, we are in a paradoxical situation in the first-past-the-post system, where the majority of the electorate may well have cast votes against the winning candidate. The proportional representation system aims to correct this anomaly.

To begin with, the proportional representation electoral system requires multiple-candidate voting districts and must allow multiple winners within the same constituency. In the *party-list* system, voters cast their votes for the party of their choice according to the list of candidates put forward in various constituencies by the party concerned. If there are four political parties, A, B, C, D, contesting, and A gets 40 per cent of the popular vote, B gets 30 per cent, C gets 20 per cent, and D gets 10 per cent, the candidates will be allotted a number of seats, according to their popular vote percentage, spread across all or several of the constituencies. So, in many constituencies, there may be no representation by parties C and D, given the fact that their vote percentages are as low as one-fifth and one-tenth, respectively, of the total. In the *single transferable vote* system, it is the candidates rather than the parties that are taken into consideration and ranked by voters, according to first preference, second preference, and so on, depending on the number of candidates in each constituency. Here, in a four-member constituency, contesting candidates (numerically many more than four) are ranked according to first preference voters, then second preference, and so on. During the counting process, candidates who get the greatest number of preferences over others are likely to be successful. Second, third and even fourth preferences will be taken into consideration, till all the four seats are filled.

In a *cumulative voting* method, voters are allowed to give more than one vote to a preferred candidate. For example, in a four-member constituency, voters can allot all four votes for a single candidate of their choice, if they do not wish to distribute them among the contesting candidates.

What are the arguments in favour of proportional representation? As mentioned earlier, there is large-scale disenfranchisement of a majority of voters, whose votes don't seem to count in a first-past-the-post system, which was finally adopted by the Indian Constitution. 'The central claim implicit here was that inequalities in political outcomes, such as those between the representation of majority and minority opinion in legislatures violated procedural equality, the equal political rights of individuals.'[52] Secondly, proportional representation allows a legislative assembly to reflect the diversity of opinion in the society in which we live. Thirdly, the proportional representative system can successfully deflect the unjust power of the majority group in a polity. Fourthly, it was believed that this system 'would make for a stronger opposition, increase the likelihood of coalition governments and necessitate greater consultation with minority political opinion, all of which would strengthen democracy'.[53] Finally, it was believed that proportional representation, which would give a voice to different sections in society, would foster greater national unity. This last point is of considerable importance because it informs us that citizenship is not merely a top-down, state conferment of a title, but a bottom-up, willing adoption of such a title.

Freedom of Religion

If we return to the 'secular triangle' (see Figures 1 and 2), we find that along with Citizenship, Freedom of Religion is a crucial element in a secular democracy. The British colonial government viewed the Hindu community and the Muslim community—with their vast multitude of sects and creeds and castes—as single units. Strangely enough, this trend has continued even after Independence in 1947.

In September 1930, M.K. Gandhi had used the phrase sarva dharma sambhaav, to indicate that all religions are equal, in the context of Hindu–Muslim unrest in the country. In a sense, this phrase implies a weak notion of state neutrality (dharma nirpekshata), where the Indian state is expected to treat all religions in the same fashion. For instance, if members of one religion are allowed to take out a procession on a public road, members of all religions should be given the freedom to take out processions on public roads.

Those who adhere to the Hindu Right's ideology are likely to disagree with such an idea of state neutrality on the ground that all religions are not equal in terms of practice. According to them, while Hinduism has been a tolerant religion, Islam and Christianity have believed in their own superiority and therefore shown intolerance towards other religions. The Gandhian notion of sarva dharma sambhaav has thus come under attack by Hindu nationalists. This was the backdrop against which the Constituent Assembly debates on minority rights (Articles 25–30) took place.

The Debates on Minority Rights

The Constituent Assembly Debates, as stated earlier, took place between December 1946 and November 1949. In the early sessions, however, the framers of the Constitution took up another important issue and attempted to protect freedom of religion as both an individual and collective right. In addition, the framers sought safeguards for minority groups by recommending reservations in the legislatures and even in the services. Since separate electorates were rejected early on, the general consensus, in the early phase, was that there would be some form of proportional representation for a period of ten years for the minorities, such as Scheduled Castes, Anglo-Indians, Muslims, Sikhs and Indian Christians, along with procedures for adult franchise and joint electorates. Special minority officers would be stationed at the Centre and in the provinces, in order to look after the interests of the different minority groups.

On 1 May 1947, Clause 13 of the Report of the Sub-Committee on Fundamental Rights[54]—a later version being Article 25 in the Indian Constitution—was moved and adopted:

> All persons are equally entitled to freedom of conscience, and the right freely to profess, practise and propagate religion, subject to public order, morality or health, and to the other provisions of this Part.

> Explanation 1—The wearing and carrying of kirpans shall be deemed to be included in the profession of the Sikh religion.
>
> Explanation 2—The above rights shall not include any economic, financial, political, or other secular activities that may be associated with religious practice.
>
> Explanation 3—The freedom of religious practice guaranteed in this clause shall not debar the State from enacting laws for the purpose of social welfare and reform, and for throwing open Hindu religious institutions of a public character to any class or section of Hindus.[55]

Clause 14—the later version being Article 26—too was moved and adopted:

> Every religious denomination or a section thereof shall have the right to manage its own affairs in matter of religion and, subject to law, to own, acquire and administer property movable and immovable, and to establish and maintain institutions for religious or charitable purposes.[56]

Then Clause 15—the later version being Article 27—was moved and adopted:

> No person may be compelled to pay taxes, the proceeds of which are specifically appropriated to further or maintain any particular religion or denomination.[57]

Clause 16—the later version being Article 28—was referred back to the Advisory Committee on Fundamental Rights, Minorities, Tribals and Excluded Areas (Advisory Committee on Minorities, in short):

> No person attending any school maintained or receiving aid out of public funds shall be compelled to take part in the religious instruction that may be given in the school or to attend religious worship held in the school or in premises attached thereto.[58]

The major debate in the Constituent Assembly was that related to religious instruction in state-aided schools. One member, Purnima Banerji, suggested that religious education in the form of elementary comparative religion be taught in educational institutions to broaden pupils' minds. Shibban Lal Saxena noted that religious instruction in educational institutions, on a voluntary basis, could be given outside working hours.[59] Reacting to these statements, K.T. Shah said that any form of religious instruction would transform educational institutions into 'a menagerie of faiths'.[60] K.M. Munshi remarked that Purnima Banerji's suggestion would be infeasible in denominational schools—like convents or madrasahs—which impart their own specific religious instruction.[61] The final version of Article 28 prohibits religious instruction in educational institutions wholly maintained and aided by the state. Other institutions that were recognized by the state and received some aid from it could allow voluntary participation in religious programmes.

The case of crucial importance concerning Article 28, or religious instruction in state educational institutions, is *Aruna Roy and Ors vs Union of India* in 2002. This case was filed when the National Curriculum Framework for School Education published by the National Council of Educational Research and Training (NCERT) added religious education to the curriculum in schools, without consulting the Central Advisory Board of Education (CABE). The court responded by differentiating between religious instruction and religious education, indicating that the latter as the study of religion was permitted. According to the court, students can be given education about religion for general awareness, that the essence of every religion is common and only practices differ. Obviously, the learned judge in this case did not deem it fit to consult the Constituent Assembly Debates on this subject.

Clause 18—later versions being Article 29 and 30—was adopted the same day, 1 May 1947, except for sub-clause (2), which was referred back to the Advisory Committee:

> (1) Minorities in every Unit shall be protected in respect of their language, script and culture, and no laws or regulations may be enacted that may operate oppressively or prejudicially in this respect.
> (2) No minority, whether based on religion, community or language shall be discriminated against in regard to the admission into State educational institutions, nor shall any religious instruction be compulsorily imposed on them.

> (3)(a) All minorities whether based on religion, community or language shall be free in any Unit to establish and administer educational institutions of their choice.
> (b) The State shall not, while providing State aid to schools, discriminate against schools under the management of minorities whether based on religion, community or language.[62]

Articles 29 and 30 permitted all citizens to conserve their language, script and culture. There were provisions for all minorities to establish and administrate educational institutions of their choice and such institutions could not be discriminated against by the state, in terms of providing aid, on the basis of their religious or linguistic identity. At the same time, these institutions could not deny admission to anyone on grounds of religion, caste or language.

Articles 25 to 30 are enshrined as justiciable rights for minority groups as well as individual members within these groups in Part III of the Indian Constitution, i.e. the section on fundamental rights. These Articles came up for discussion once more on 7 December 1948.[63] The discussion 'crystallized around two positions'. Lokanath Misra expressed the opinion that they would weaken the unity of India by granting too many concessions to minority groups. Damodar Swarup Seth felt that cultural and educational rights for the minorities would promote communalism and needed to be put in the non-justiciable Directive Principles section of the Constitution.[64]

At the other end of the ideological spectrum were members like Z.H. Lari, who were furious that Clause 18(1) had been changed as follows: 'Any section of the citizens residing in the territory of India or any part thereof, having a distinct language, script and culture of its own shall have the right to conserve the same.' This finally became sub-clause (1) of Article 29 in the Indian Constitution. Lari's point was that the change in phraseology simply implied that any citizen had a right to use his or her script or language privately—that was stating the obvious! The real question was whether the state was going to pay for the promotion of the language, script and culture of different minority communities, as had been promised in the earlier version of Clause 18(1).[65]

Sub-clause (2), which later became sub-clause (2) of Article 29 in the Indian Constitution, as recommended by the Advisory Committee, read: 'No minority, whether based on religion, community or language shall be discriminated against in regard to admission into State educational institutions.' This was changed by an amendment moved by Pandit Thakurdas Bhargava and adopted by the Assembly. It now read: 'No citizen shall be denied admission into any educational institution maintained by the State or receiving aid out of State funds on grounds only of religion, race, caste, language or any of them.'[66] The net result was that specific provisions for religious minorities had become somewhat diluted and were now applicable to all citizens in a general sense.

By July 1947, the question of the partition of the subcontinent into two states, India and Pakistan, had been decided. On 27 August 1947, the first Report by the Advisory Committee on Minorities was tabled for discussion in the Constituent Assembly. Vallabhbhai Patel had accepted on 8 August 1947 most of the recommendations in the Report on Minority Rights. On 27 August 1947, he stated that 'we have thought fit to agree to reservation in proportion to the population of the minorities'. However, there wasn't much to rejoice about, as far as the minorities were concerned, given the many caveats that were in place. 'In August, the Advisory Committee modified these safeguards by rejecting any reservation for the minorities in the government services, by holding over the question of reserved legislative seats for the Sikhs and by allowing reserved representation for Indian Christians in the Central legislature and in the provincial legislatures of Madras and Bombay alone.'[67]

On the following day, 28 August 1947, Clause 5 of the Draft Constitution read as follows: 'The minorities for whom representation has been reserved will be allotted seats on their population ratio and there shall be no weightage for any community.' D.H. Chandrasekharaiya tried to move an amendment to the effect that provision should be made for conducting all elections on the system of proportional representation by a single transferable vote, or, if not adopted, by a single non-transferable vote. The attempt drew another member, Ajit Prasad Jain, to comment that this proposed amendment would bring in a system of separate electorates through the back door. Sardar Patel seemed to have suddenly found the idea of proportional representation unsavoury: 'The amendment that was moved does not suit our conditions, because we are now going to make an experiment of having elections by adult franchise, which will bring on the rolls millions of ignorant voters. That being the case, the complicated system that has been suggested will be absolutely unsuited to us. I do not propose to accept it.'[68] There was no more discussion on the proposed amendment, which was anyway 'negatived'.[69] Clause 5, however, was adopted. In the Indian Constitution, Article 8 provided the right to vote to all adult citizens.

On the same day, K.T.M. Ahmed Ibrahim Sahib Bahadur reflected the sombre mood of the Assembly in the aftermath of the Partition: 'Left to myself I would have wished that this Report on the Rights of Minorities was considered at a time when this country was free from all passion and the heat of the moment has subsided and tied down, but unfortunately it has been taken up now... The only purpose is that the views and opinions of the minorities and the other communities may be reflected on the floor of the House in a proper manner'.[70]

Soon after Independence on 15 August 1947, rioting had started in India and Pakistan. Hindus were attacked in the new state of Pakistan and consequently fled to India after abandoning their property and businesses, and they harboured hatred and anger towards Muslims in general. In fact, Kazi Syed Karimuddin felt that, with the creation of Pakistan and the resultant resentment on the part of the Hindu majority, it was important that Muslims in India would not be made a scapegoat by society and the state. He wished to add clause (4) to Article 14 in the Draft Constitution, which was to become Article 20 in the Indian Constitution. The phrasing of Article 20 is as follows: 'No person shall be convicted of any offence except for violation of a law in force at the time of the commission of the act charged as an offence, nor be subjected to a penalty greater than that which might have been inflicted under the law at the time of the commission of the offence.'

The proposed clause (4) read: 'The right of the people to be secure in their persons, houses, papers and effects against unreasonable searches and seizures shall not be violated and no warrants shall issue but upon probable cause supported by oath or affirmation and particularly describing the place to be searched and the persons or things to be seized.'[71] Since there was some confusion as to whether the ayes or the noes had it, the voting on this amendment was postponed, on the advice of Jawaharlal Nehru.

The Volte-Face

In the Draft Constitution of early 1948, there were a few special provisions for reservation of minority communities.

While Articles 292 and 294 provided for proportional representation of religious minority groups on a joint electorate basis in central and regional legislatures, Article 296 provided for reservation in the services and Article 299 provided for the appointment of special officers to oversee the safeguards for protecting the interests of minority groups.

On 8 November 1948, reservation in services was done away with for religious minorities. Z.H. Lari made the impassioned plea: 'It is possible in a single-member constituency to disenfranchise even a minority extending to 49 per cent... The only means of safeguarding minorities is by adopting the system of proportional representation... Take away the reservation from the Legislature and for God's sake give us reservation in the services... You concede reservations [in the services] to Anglo-Indians but you deny it to the Muslims. Why this discrimination?'[72] Lari's speech drew a reaction from Vishwambhar Dayal Tripathi: 'What did your leaders do in Pakistan?' To this, Lari responded: 'I have not mortgaged my rights to Pakistan. I stand here as a citizen of India. What Pakistan does or does not do is not my concern.' The meeting was then called to order by the Vice-President.

The matter did not rest there, as more members started speaking out in favour of the proportional representation system. On 4 January 1949, Kazi Syed Karimuddin pointed out: 'The one pervading evil of democracy is the tyranny

of the majority that succeeds in carrying elections... The common system of representation perpetuates the danger and the only remedy is proportional representation... I plead that if proportional representation is guaranteed, the reservation of seats even on religious grounds must go... [S] eparation, communalism and isolation must disappear from the body politic of India, but we cannot ignore the existing conditions in the country. We find that there is a movement for the establishment of a Hindu Raj. We find that there is an RSS [Rashtriya Swayamsevak Sangh] organization also in the country. In view of this, we have to proceed cautiously and gradually, and therefore we have to find out a way that communalism must go, and the minorities must be represented in the legislatures.'[73]

K.T. Shah, Mahboob Ali Baig Sahib Bahadur and Hukam Singh also spoke in favour of proportional representation for minority groups. While arguing in favour of proportional representation by a single transferable vote, Mahboob Ali Baig Sahib Bahadur expressed some thoughts against majoritarianism: 'Can you think of any parliamentary democracy where there is no opposition? Unless there is opposition...the danger of its turning into a Fascist body is there.'[74] In response to Kazi Syed Karimuddin's proposed amendment concerning proportional representation by the cumulative voting method, Dr Ambedkar expressed his misgivings on the ground that the proportional representation system 'presupposes literacy on a large scale...

In fact, it presupposes that every voter shall be literate, at least to the extent of being in a position to know the numerals, and to be in a position to mark them on a ballot paper'.[75] It seemed, then, that the door to the proportional representation system was being shut in favour of the British parliamentary system of adult franchise and 'first past the post'. However, there would still be reservations for all minority groups in the legislatures, which had already been moved and approved in the Constituent Assembly.

On 25 May 1949, Sardar Patel tabled the Report of the Advisory Committee, comprising Jawaharlal Nehru, Dr B.R. Ambedkar, Sardar Patel and K.M. Munshi, in the Constituent Assembly. In a stunning move, the Minorities Sub-Committee had taken 'the unprecedented step of dropping the provision of reserved seats' for religious minorities,[76] even though it had been approved earlier by the Assembly. Sardar Patel provided the rationale for doing away with all reservation for Muslims in the legislatures by claiming that the Muslim members in the Assembly were not in accord with one another and had put forward 'the plea that all these reservations must disappear'. To this, Mohammed Ismail Khan responded that it was unfair to take the opinions of a few Muslim members in the Assembly as being representative of all the members of the community: 'Now if the majority community or the party in power [wants] to do away with any of the safeguards, that is one thing. But I submit that it is not fair to place the responsibility for doing away with such safeguards on the shoulders of the minority... How can a community help being a Muslim community or a Christian community? It is not a joke for the minority communities always to be courting disfavour and criticism from the majority community.'[77]

Z.H. Lari's speech on the same subject was interrupted in the middle by H.V. Kamath, who posed the hackneyed question: 'Why did you demand Pakistan?' Lari responded: 'You say you regard me as an integral part of the nation. But the moment you raise such criticisms you give away the whole show. You show that you do not regard me as a part of the whole, that you are still harbouring old suspicions.' Lari went on to say that, by conceding reservations to the Scheduled Castes, the Advisory Committee revealed that it was not mindful of the interests of the Muslim community.[78]

The Indian Constitution provided reservation to the Anglo-Indian community in the Lok Sabha (Article 331) and in the legislative assemblies (Article 333). Similarly, it provided reservation to Scheduled Castes and Scheduled Tribes in the Lok Sabha (Article 330) and in the legislative assemblies (Article 332). However, on 10 August 1950, nearly eight months after the Constitution was established as guiding the Indian Republic, President Rajendra Prasad issued the Scheduled Castes Order, whereby converts to Christianity or Islam were no longer deemed to be

Scheduled Castes, while a circular of the Home Ministry in 1959 explicitly stated that converts to these religions could not avail themselves of the benefits of reservation.

The religious minorities were placed completely outside the purview of reservations. Jawaharlal Nehru stated that political reservations would isolate the religious minorities from mainstream politics. Dr H.C. Mookherjee, Chairman of the Minorities Sub-Committee in the Advisory Committee, pointed out that, in the interests of building a secular and a strong nation, reservation of seats for religious minorities had to be abolished. Since the Assembly had passed fundamental rights, which guarantee religious, cultural and educational safeguards for the minorities, why was there any need for political safeguards like providing reservation in the legislatures?[79]

Shefali Jha refers to the trade-off between reserved seats and fundamental rights for religious minorities: 'Each of the representative models suggested for forestalling majoritarianism—for example, proportional representation or reserved seats for minorities—were rejected; but instead of trying to shore up or strengthen representation by proposing some alternative anti-majoritarian representative scheme, the solution proposed to allay the fears of minority groups was a set of rights which included not merely individual rights but a few collective rights for minorities as well.'[80]

On 14 October 1949, when political safeguards for

the Sikh community were withdrawn, Hukam Singh spoke bitterly of the 'broken promises' of the Congress party. Sardar Patel expressed his irritation with respect to the reactions of the different religious minority groups to the sudden withdrawal of political safeguards: 'What is the use of charging the Congress with having broken promises? Do not break the promises that you have given, and do not charge others with breach of promises.' He then went on to say, 'I know that the atmosphere so far as the Muslims are concerned is not quite as happy as it should be... The Congress is not responsible for this. If there had been no Partition, perhaps we would have been able to settle our differences.'[81]

Perhaps the question that needs to be asked here is, what caused senior leaders to change their mind about providing political safeguards to Indian Muslims? Sardar Patel blames the trauma of Partition for creating the fear of further fragmentation of the country in the mind of the nationalists. But as Rochana Bajpai informs us, there could be other reasons as well. She says, '[I]n the nationalist vocabulary, there was a normative deficit in the case of *group representation* as such, and this enables us to understand better the retraction of legislative quotas for religious minorities during Constitution making.'[82] This was particularly true of leaders like Jawaharlal Nehru, who—like a true liberal of his time—valued individual rights over group rights. In late 1948, he stated that 'while it is our bounden duty to do everything we can to give full opportunity to every minority or group and to raise every backward group or class, I do not think it will be a right thing to go the way this country has gone in the past by creating barriers and by calling for protection. As a matter of fact nothing can protect such a minority or a group less than a barrier which separates it from the majority'.[83]

Despite Nehru's misgivings about group rights, the Indian Constitution had provisions for caste-based reservations (Articles 15, 16, 330, 332), religious minority rights (Articles 25, 26, 27, 28, 29, 30), and special status for Jammu and Kashmir (Article 370, revoked on 5 August 2019) and the north-eastern states (Article 371). Four decades on, by the 1990s, all these rights would be viewed by liberal scholars with the new lens of 'multiculturalism' that took the form of cultural rights, special representation and regional autonomy for certain previously disadvantaged or minority groups in the polity. In retrospect, one could say that the Indian Constitution was far ahead of its time. However, the general perspective among Indian nationalists like Nehru, Patel and Ambedkar in 1950 was one of classic liberalism, which plainly favoured individual rights over group rights.

Furthermore, it is interesting to note the various ideologies expressed during the Constituent Assembly Debates—the social-democratic vision of members like Jawaharlal Nehru, the liberal-democratic Ambedkarite vision, the quasi-communitarian Gandhi vision, the radical egalitarianism of members like K.T. Shah, and the Hindutva vision of members like Syama Prasad Mukherjee.[84] Given this medley composition, it is hardly surprising that after Partition of the country in August 1947, there were sharp exchanges between a few Hindu and Muslim members, and an unfortunate tendency on the part of the former to blame all Muslims for the creation of Pakistan.

Answering the question, 'What is a Constitution?' B. Pattabhi Sitaramayya pointed out that 'it is a grammar of politics, if you like, it is a compass to the political mariner. However good it may be, by itself it is inanimate, it is insensitive, and it cannot work by itself. It is of use to us only in the measure in which we are able to use it, because it has tremendous reserve force, and everything depends upon the manner in which we approach it'. Then going on to give the example of the joint electorate in the context of working the new Constitution, Sitaramayya voiced the anxiety of most members in the Assembly: 'We have established the joint electorate. Have we discharged our duty? Shall we leave the electorate to do what it pleases? ... Is it possible for [Muslims] to win a single seat by their own unaided strength, without our cooperation? It is a gentlemen's [*sic*] agreement that we have entered into, a terrible responsibility that we have taken upon our shoulders, when we asked them to give up their reservations and their separate electorates. We have to find as many representatives from the Muslim community through the medium of the joint electorate as would have been their legitimate share, if they had their separate electorates. Even so with the Indian Christians and others'.[85]

With all reservations withdrawn, the religious minorities were left with the constitutional provisions of Articles 25–30:

Article 25

(1) Subject to public order, morality and health and to other provisions of this Part [i.e. Part III], all persons are equally entitled to freedom of conscience and the right freely to profess, practise and propagate religion.
(2) Nothing in this article shall affect the operation of any existing law or prevent the state from making any law—

(a) regulating or restricting any economic, financial, political or other secular activity which may be associated with religious practice;
(b) providing for social welfare reform or the throwing open of Hindu religious institutions of a public character to all classes of and sections of Hindus.

Article 26

Subject to public order, morality and health, every religious denomination or any section thereof shall have the right—

(a) to establish and maintain institutions for religious and charitable purposes;

(b) to manage its own affairs in matters of religion;

(c) to own and acquire movable and immovable property; and

(d) to administer such property in accordance with the law.

Article 27

No person shall be compelled to pay any taxes, the proceeds of which are specifically appropriated in payment of expenses for the promotion or maintenance of any particular religion or religious denomination.

Article 28

(1) No religious instruction shall be provided in any educational institution wholly maintained out of State funds.

(2) Nothing in clause (1) shall apply to an educational institution which is administered by the State but has been established under any endowment or trust which requires that religious instruction shall be imparted in such institution.

(3) No person attending any educational institution recognised by the State or receiving aid out of State funds shall be required to take part in any religious instruction that may be imparted in such institution or to attend any religious worship that may be conducted in such institution or in any premises attached thereto unless

such person or, if such person is a minor, his guardian has given his consent thereto.

Article 29

(1) Any section of the citizens residing in the territory of India or any part thereof having a distinct language, script or culture of its own shall have the right to conserve the same.
(2) No citizen shall be denied admission into any educational institution maintained by the State or receiving aid out of State funds on grounds only of religion, race, caste, language or any of them.

Article 30

(1) All minorities, whether based on religion or language, shall have the right to establish and administer educational institutions of their choice.
(1A) In making any law providing for the compulsory acquisition of any property of an educational institution established and administered by a minority, referred to in clause (1), the State shall ensure that the amount fixed by or determined under such law for the acquisition of such property is such as would not restrict or abrogate the right guaranteed under that clause.
(2) The state shall not, in granting aid to educational institutions, discriminate against any educational institution on the ground that it is under the management of a minority, whether based on religion or language.

Since there were so many unresolved issues during the making of the Indian Constitution, these were later passed on to the judiciary for some sort of final resolution. Broadly speaking, the 'earthly judges' that John Locke had referred to in *A Letter Concerning Toleration* were called upon—or took it upon themselves—to make pronouncements on religious matters and to test the truth claims of different religions. The judgements and their consequences constitute the subject matter of the next chapter.

Chapter III

Judging Secularism

It was the 42nd Amendment to the Indian Constitution in 1976 which explicitly established India as a secular state in the Preamble to the Constitution, by adding the words 'socialist' and 'secular': 'We, the people of India, having solemnly resolved to constitute India into a Sovereign Socialist Secular Democratic Republic and to secure to all its citizens: Justice, social, economic and political; Liberty of thought, expression, belief, faith and worship; Equality of status and opportunity; and to promote among them all Fraternity, assuring the dignity of the individual and the unity and integrity of the Nation; In our Constituent Assembly, this twenty-sixth of November, 1949, do hereby adopt, enact and give to ourselves this Constitution.'

What was the rationale for the government passing the 42nd Amendment? The landmark judgement of the thirteen-judge constitutional bench in the 1973 case,

Kesavananda Bharati vs State of Kerala, concerning the imposition of state restrictions on the petitioner's property, found disfavour with Indira Gandhi's government. In a divided verdict of 7–6 in the *Kesavananda Bharati* case, the court conceded that Parliament had wide powers, but it did not have the power to destroy the basic structure of the fundamental rights, by making these subservient to the directive principles, which are non-justiciable, in the name of establishing a welfare state. In this context, the judges also declared that secularism was a fundamental law of the land.

The *Kesavananda Bharati* judgement was the reason for Mrs Gandhi passing the infamous 42nd Amendment, which stripped the Supreme Court of many of its powers and tried to direct the Indian polity towards a system of parliamentary sovereignty. In other words, this amendment devalued the Indian Constitution and democratic practice, by giving sweeping powers to the Prime Minister's Office. The 42nd Amendment also changed the description of India in the Preamble from 'sovereign democratic republic' in the 1950 Constitution to 'sovereign, socialist, secular democratic republic'.

Even prior to the 42nd Amendment, judges in courts had referred to the 'secular' nature of the polity in their judgements. The Supreme Court's first use of the word 'secularism' was in the 1962 judgement in *Sardar Syedna Taher Saifuddin Saheb vs State of Bombay*, concerning the invalidity of excommunication of a member of the Dawoodi

Bohra community. Justice N. Rajagopala Ayyangar explained that Articles 25 and 26 'embody the principle of religious toleration... [B]esides, they serve to emphasize the secular nature of Indian democracy, which the founding fathers considered to be the very basis of the Constitution'.[86]

Let us, then, consider each of the clauses in Articles 25 and 26 of the Indian Constitution with respect to some landmark judgements.

Dissecting Article 25—Sub-Clause (1)

'Subject to public order, morality and health and to other provisions of this Part, all persons are equally entitled to freedom of conscience and the right freely to profess, practise and propagate religion,' states the sub-clause.

Since Independence, several cases concerning the propagation of religion have come before the courts. This is hardly surprising, considering the acrimonious debates on religious conversion during the Constituent Assembly Debates, where it was finally decided not to include the banning of forcible conversions in the section on fundamental rights, but to leave it to the legislatures and the courts to decide on the matter, on a case-by-case basis (see Chapter I).

After the Madhya Pradesh state government introduced legislation in the 1960s to curb 'forcible' religious conversions, an extremely important case, *Rev Stanislaus vs State of Madhya Pradesh*, came before the Supreme Court in 1977.

Rev Stanislaus, a Christian priest from Madhya Pradesh, had refused to register the conversions in his parish with the state government, as was required by the new legislation. Consequently, he was arrested under the Act and faced criminal prosecution. Rev Stanislaus, for his part, challenged the validity of the legislation on the ground that it violated sub-clause (1) of Article 25, which allowed the propagation of religion. However, the five-judge bench ruled that the Madhya Pradesh state government was well within its rights to pass anti-conversion legislation, if religious conversions created, or were in danger of creating, public disorder. Since the definition of 'public disorder' is very broad, it stands to reason that the state's power to legislate is also very broad.[87]

In fact, Chief Justice A.N. Ray, who presided over the case, came up with a rather curious argument concerning the actual meaning of Article 25(1): 'What the Article grants is not the right to convert another person to one's own religion by an exposition of its tenets. It has to be remembered that Article 25(1) guarantees freedom of conscience to every citizen, and not merely to the followers of one particular religion, and that, in turn, postulates that there is no fundamental right to convert another person to one's own religion, because if a person purposely undertakes the conversion of another person to his religion, as distinguished from his effort to transmit or spread the tenets of his religion, that would impinge on the "freedom of conscience" guaranteed to all the citizens of the country alike.'

Political scientist Ronojoy Sen informs us that 'the Stanislaus judgment has...not been reconsidered by a larger bench and continues to be the last word on the meaning of the right to propagate'.[88]

Would the courts decide the *Stanislaus* case today very differently, in the light of the 2017 judgement in the *Justice K.S. Puttaswamy and Anr vs Union of India and Ors* case? In the landmark *Puttaswamy* judgement, the right to privacy is protected as a fundamental right under Article 14 (equality of all citizens), Article 19 (freedom of expression) and Article 21 (right to life) of the Constitution of India. Could we now say that Rev Stanislaus had a right to privacy when he exercised his agency as an adult and chose not to reveal the changed faith of his parishioners to the state authorities in Madhya Pradesh? Those who propagate religion, as well as those who convert to another religion, could well be subjected to physical and psychological torture by prejudicial state authorities. This is sufficient reason for protecting the right to privacy of all citizens in any polity. However, we know from recent experience, whether it concerns the protection of the identity of minors under the POCSO (Protection of Children from Sexual Offences) Act or the protection of personal data, that the right to privacy of Indian citizens is honoured in the breach rather than the observance.

Dissecting Article 25—Sub-Clause (2)(a)

'[Nothing in this article shall affect the operation of any existing law or prevent the state from making any law] regulating or restricting any economic, financial, political or other secular activity which may be associated with religious practice...' reads Article 25(2)(a).

The ground-breaking case here is the 1954 case—*Commissioner, Hindu Religious Endowments, Madras vs Sri Lakshmindra Thirtha Swamiar of Sri Shirur Mutt*, commonly known as the *Shirur Mutt* case. This case constituted a direct challenge to the Madras Hindu Religious and Charitable Endowment (HRCE) Act of 1951,[89] where the petitioner, the *mahant* of the Shirur Mutt, claimed that interference by the HRCE in the management of the Mutt constituted a violation of Article 26, namely, the right to establish and maintain institutions for religious and charitable purposes; to manage its own affairs in matters of religion; to own and acquire movable and immovable property; and to administer such property in accordance with the law.[90]

Justice B.K. Mukherjea, who wrote the judgement in the *Shirur Mutt* case, pointed out that 'what constitutes the essential part of a religion is primarily to be ascertained with reference to the doctrines of that religion itself'. Justice Mukherjea famously made a distinction between the 'essential' and 'non-essential' parts of a religion. Article 26 gives any religious institution complete autonomy to manage its own affairs in matters of religion, and protects the essential part of religion, including rituals, beliefs, superstitions, and forms of worship. In fact, Justice Mukherjea made it clear that '[n]o outside authority has any right to say that these are not essential parts of religion, and it is not open to the secular authority of the State to restrict or prohibit them in any manner they like under the guise of administering the trust estate'. But, at the same time, Justice Mukherjea averred, the state had a right to interfere in the non-religious affairs of religious institutions, namely, their economic or political aspects, or indeed any other aspect which affected public order, health or morality.

Since the *Shirur Mutt* judgement had validated the Madras HRCE Act of 1951, other states soon passed similar legislation. While Justice Mukherjea had considerably broadened the ambit of religious belief and worship in Article 26, he could not quite bridge the inherent contradiction between Articles 25 and 26, given his rationale and support for explicit state interference, in the context of Article 25(2)(a), in 'non-essential' matters of religious institutions. The question is, who decides what is essential to a religion? Legal expert Rajeev Dhavan informs us, 'What was at issue was not just an offence to religious sentiment, but the institutional right of religious endowments to manage their own affairs. By treating vast areas of state intervention as a matter of course and therefore acceptable, the autonomy of many institutions was undermined.' Dhavan also warns us: 'Although the Srirur Math [*sic*] case has been commended for its balance and objectivity, it has always been an invitation to both judicial statesmanship and mischief.'[91]

Once judges take it upon themselves to define the essential and non-essential features of any religion, the judgements are likely to reflect certain biases and prejudices. In the 1958 case, *Mohd Hanif Quareshi vs State of Bihar*, the petitioner challenged the ban on sale of cattle for slaughter as being unconstitutional. In 1956, the Bihar government had passed the Bihar Preservation and Improvement of Animals Act, which banned the slaughter of all categories of bovine cattle. According to the petitioner, this Act violated the right of Muslims to practise their religion, and offended their religion, as the sacrifice of a cow on specific days was enjoined by Islam. The court, however, ruled that 'slaughtering of cows on Bakr Id is neither essential to nor necessarily required as part of the religious ceremony. An optional religious practice is not covered by Article 25(1). On the contrary, it is common knowledge that the cow and its progeny i.e. bull, bullocks and calves are worshipped by Hindus on specified days'. Apparently, here, the customary practices of the majority community take precedence over those of minority communities.

In the most recent case, on 15 March 2022, the Karnataka High Court noted that wearing the *hijab*, the headscarf, did not constitute an essential practice of the Islamic faith. According to Dushyant Dave, former president of the Supreme Court Bar Association, the honourable judge in this case who used the 'essentiality' test in the 1954 *Shirur Mutt* judgement, had misunderstood the broad framework employed by Justice B.K. Mukherjea.[92] In his 1954 judgement, Justice Mukherjea had said: 'It would not be correct to say that religion is nothing else but a doctrine or belief. A religion may not only lay down a code of ethical rules for its followers to accept, it might prescribe rituals and observances, ceremonies and modes of worship which are regarded as integral parts of religion, and these forms and observances might extend even to matters of food and dress.'

At the beginning of January 2022, several Muslim girls wearing the hijab had been denied entry into Karnataka state-run schools and colleges on the ground that the hijab violated the institutions' policy of wearing a specific uniform. In a counter move, a few Hindu students demanded the right to wear saffron scarves. Petitions were filed by the aggrieved Muslim girls in the Karnataka High Court under Articles 14[93] and 25(1). Already, on 10 February 2022, the High Court had issued an interim order restraining students from wearing religious attire of any kind. In its judgement of 15 March 2022, the honourable judges took it upon themselves to restrict and prohibit a religious practice that was considered essential by the petitioners, that had been tolerated by the same educational institutions in previous years, and that had been upheld as essential practice in the 1954 *Shirur Mutt* case.

The decision regarding essential and non-essential religious practices has often been arbitrary. In the 1983 case involving the Ananda Margis, *Commissioner of Police vs Acharya Jagdishwaranand Avadhuta*, the court refused to view the *tandava* dance (carrying lethal weapons and human skulls) as an essential part of their religious practice. The court reasoned that the 'Ananda Marga as a religious order is of recent origin and *tandava* dance as a part of religious rites of that order is still more recent. It is doubtful as to whether in such circumstances *tandava* dance can be taken as an essential religious rite of the Ananda Margis'.

Indeed, our 'earthly judges', however learned they may be, often do not even see eye to eye on rather similar cases. In 1983, in *S.P. Mittal vs Union of India*, the judgement was that Sri Aurobindo's teachings comprised a philosophy and not a religion, despite his followers' belief that the teachings constituted a religion. In the 1995 *Bramchari Sidheswar Shai and Ors vs State of West Bengal* case, the court ruled that the followers of the Ramakrishna Math may be considered as a part—or denomination—of the Hindu religion.

In the 1990s, there were several cases centred on major Hindu temples in various parts of the country, like Tirupathi, Vaishno Devi, Jagannath and Kashi Vishwanath. Justice K. Ramaswamy, who presided over these cases, argued firmly in favour of state intervention in the regulation of the administration of these temples: 'Secularism, being a basic feature of the Constitution, the Constitution does not permit the State to interfere with the management of religious affairs of any religion or denomination. But the State has power to interfere with the same for proper supervision and efficient management of religious institution or endowment which is secular in its character.' This excerpt from Justice K. Ramaswamy's judgement on the 1997 case, *Bhuri Nath and Ors vs State of Jammu & Kashmir*, also known as the *Vaishno Devi* case, led a few legal experts to comment: 'If the regulatory impetus provided by Justice B.K. Mukherjea in the fifties was enlarged by Justice Gajendragadkar [see next section] in the sixties, the latest judgments of Justice K. Ramaswamy have enthusiastically supported the "nationalization" of some of India's greatest shrines.'[94]

It must be remembered that state intervention, including appropriation, in the economic and financial affairs of religious institutions began in European countries in 1648, with the signing of the Treaty of Westphalia. The process was continued during the French Revolution and after. The question in India, given its extremely unequal society, is whether the huge wealth and income accrued by several religious institutions are liable to be taxed and regulated by state authorities, in an attempt to curb corrupt practices.[95] The answer will depend on the definition of secularism in India. On the one hand, one could view secularism largely in terms of the separation of state and religion, which is primarily relegated to the private realm, and decry any state intervention as a contravention of this principle. On the other, one could recognize the public nature of religion and understand both the demands made by different religions on the state and the moral right of the state to intervene in non-religious matters of religious institutions on a principled basis. It is only when a state institution like the judiciary goes beyond this brief of intervention on a principled or constitutional basis, and attempts to define or interpret religious concepts subjectively, that it is likely to face criticism.

Dissecting Article 25—Sub-Clause (2)(b)

'[Nothing in this article shall affect the operation of any existing law or prevent the state from making any law]... providing for social welfare reform or the throwing open of Hindu religious institutions of a public character to all classes of and sections of Hindus', says this sub-clause.

A crucial part of the nationalist movement, the Vaikom Satyagraha, in the 1920s, was a social protest against caste discrimination and untouchability in the kingdom of Travancore in Kerala. The social protest against caste-based discrimination, especially in Hindu temples which refused to allow untouchables into their premises, took other forms in the 1930s.

In 1947, the Madras Presidency had enacted the Madras Temple Entry Authorisation Act. One of the early cases pertaining to temple entry of Dalits (former Untouchables) was the 1957 case, *Sri Venkataramana Devaru vs State of Mysore*. The argument of the head priest of the Gowda Saraswath Brahmin temple at Moolky for not allowing Dalits was that the Sri Venkataramana temple itself was a private institution and therefore beyond the scope of Article 17 of the Indian Constitution, which states: 'Untouchability is abolished and its practice in any form is forbidden. The enforcement of any disability arising out of Untouchability shall be an offence punishable in accordance with law.'

According to the head priest, even if the Moolky temple was a public institution, Article 26 gave the temple authorities complete autonomy and protection from state interference. Justice T.L. Venkatarama Aiyar, however, 'ruled that the temple entry legislation was in fact only eliminating a discrepancy between Agamic injunctions [or Hindu Brahmanical texts that uphold the importance of temple rituals] and customary practice... Ultimately, the decision in *Devaru* upheld the status of the Agamas as authoritative determination of correct religious practice, while indicating that, properly interpreted, they did not exclude Dalits.'[96] In this case, the Agamas had already provided rules about the hierarchical location of different castes, including Dalits, within the Vaishnavite temple. With the principle of equality implicit in Article 25(2)(b), there could be no more such hierarchical restrictions regarding the location of different castes within a Hindu temple.

What was significant about the *Devaru* case was that Justice Aiyar confined his comments on the case to examining the validity of the Madras Temple Entry Authorisation Act of 1947, along with a reading of the statutes made under clause (2)(b) to Article 25, in order to come to the conclusion that there were exceptions to the freedoms guaranteed by Articles 25 and 26. Another well-known judge, Justice P.B. Gajendragadkar, while depending on the 'essentiality' argument inherent in the *Shirur Mutt* case, took it in a completely new direction.

In a 1961 case, *Durgah Committee vs Syed Hussain Ali*, Justice Gajendragadkar had referred to the essential part of religion, but also—for the first time—tried to rationalize religion by distinguishing between superstitious beliefs and religious practice: '[E]ven practices though religious may have sprung from merely superstitious beliefs and may in that sense be extraneous and unessential accretions to religion itself.' While Justice Aiyar had tried to understand the scriptures of the religion in the *Devaru* case, Justice Gajendragadkar had already made up his mind about what was authentic and what was inauthentic about the religion in the *Durgah Committee* case, thereby drastically limiting the scope of Article 26 for the petitioners.

The landmark case in 1966, presided over by Justice Gajendragadkar, was *Sastri Yagnapurushadji vs Muldas Bhudardas Vaishya*, also known as the *Satsangi* case. The Satsangis were followers of Swaminarayan (1780–1830).

They claimed that their cult did not fall under the purview of the Bombay Harijan[97] Temple Entry Act of 1948. The Satsangis claimed that they only worshipped Swaminarayan as a god, and not any Hindu deity, whose worship anyway is anathema to the cult followers. Furthermore, Satsangis had to go through an initiation rite before being accepted by the Swaminarayan cult. Justice Gajendragadkar made the following pronouncement on this cult: 'The Satsangi's apprehension about the pollution of the temple is founded on superstition, ignorance and complete misunderstanding of the true teachings of Hinduism and the real significance of the tenets and philosophy taught by Swami Narayan himself.'

Instead of confining himself to the Bombay Harijan Temple Entry Act of 1948 or to Article 25(2)(b), the honourable Justice Gajendragadkar decided to do the impossible—define Hinduism. Admitting the difficulty in doing so, the learned judge started out by stating that Hinduism 'is a way of life and nothing more', and taking inspiration from Sarvepalli Radhakrishnan's 1926 Upton Lectures, he attempted to portray Hinduism as an all-inclusive religion.

Ronojoy Sen explains the later political implications in the courts of depicting Hinduism as a way of life.[98] In 2005, the judge in *Bal Patil vs Union of India* ruled that the 'so-called minority communities like Sikhs and Jains...have throughout been treated as part of the wider

Hindu community which has different sects, sub-sects, faiths, modes of worship and religious philosophies'. The honourable judge went on to deprecate minority rights in general, and called for a government policy of secularism, construed as 'equal treatment of religions'—or at least the inclusion of 'minor' religions under the broad rubric of Hinduism, which is, after all, 'a way of life'.

In the 1996 'Hindutva' case (mentioned below), *Dr Ramesh Yeshwant Prabhoo vs Prabhakar Kashinath Kunte*, Justice J.S. Verma referred to the definition of Hinduism in the *Satsangi* case, and proceeded to conflate Hinduism with Hindutva, which he defined as 'a way of life'—a definition that, according to him, could not be equated with 'narrow fundamentalist Hindu religious bigotry'. Not surprisingly, Justice Verma's judgement had enormous repercussions. Ronojoy Sen informs us, 'Since then it has become standard practice for the BJP and other Hindu nationalist groups to refer to the Court ruling to justify the inclusiveness of Hindutva.'[99]

Even more contentious than the judgements on Articles 25 and 26 have been the judgements concerning the minority rights, Articles 29 and 30, in the Indian Constitution.

Minority Rights in the Constitution

Articles 25–30 of our Constitution were all supposed to be 'minority rights'. As we know from Chapter II, some crucial changes were made to Articles 25 and 26, in particular, so that they lost their 'minority' character and became applicable to all communities in India. Articles 29 and 30 are known generally as 'minority rights', but there has been a fair amount of resistance even here, on the part of judges, to the idea of giving special concessions to minorities. There has been a consistent tendency over the years—especially over the past decade—to devalue the Urdu language as well as regional languages, by positing the Hindi language as a 'national' language, whereas Hindi is no more than one official language among several.

In terms of court cases, however, Article 30(1) has been the most contentious.[100] The Kerala Education Bill, 1957 had mandated that neither state-run schools nor private schools should charge tuition fee from students in primary schools. The Bill was an attempt to legislate on Directive Principle Article 45, which mandated that the government provide free and compulsory education to all children up to the age of 14 years. However, Justice S.R. Das pronounced the majority judgement in the 1958 case,[101] by pointing out that it was impossible for a minority institution to run without charging any fee. In his 'counter-constitutional' dissenting judgement, Justice Venkatarama Aiyar said that 'there is no justification for putting on Article 30(1) a construction which would put the minorities in a more favoured position than the majority communities'.

Interestingly, there have been echoes of these opposing points of view in later judgements. In *St Xavier's College*

Society, Ahmedabad vs State of Gujarat, 1974, Chief Justice A.N. Ray unambiguously held that the rights conferred under Article 30(1) are confined to linguistic and religious minorities and 'no other section of citizens of India has such a right'. On the other hand, in *TMA Pai Foundation vs State of Karnataka*, 2002, Chief Justice B.N. Kirpal declared his take on Article 30(1): '[T]he essence of Article 30(1) is to ensure equal treatment between the majority and minority institutions... Laws of the land, including rules and regulations, must apply equally to the majority institutions as well as to the minority institutions.' The judgement in this case more or less negated the very meaning of 'minority rights'.

Judges continued to vacillate on the question of Article 30(1). The main question here was as follows: Were rights confined to linguistic and religious minorities, or were they applicable to majority and minority communities alike? If the 2003 case, *Islamic Academy of Education vs State of Karnataka*, decided in favour of the former view, the 2005 case, *P.A. Inamdar vs State of Maharashtra* favoured—with a few caveats—the latter view of equal rights for all communities. Since Article 30(1) is open to either interpretation by judges, it remains a somewhat unresolved issue in the courts.

Quite apart from the constitutional provisions for protecting religious rights of all citizens, including religious minorities, there have been several egregious violations of the Representation of the People Act during elections in this country. The judgements on many of these cases, ranging from the mid-1970s to the present day, have often been on the side of the perpetrators of these violations.

'Hindutva' Cases

Once the Constitution validated the secular nature of the Indian polity in 1976, it was easy for judges to adjudicate on cases related to electoral practice. However, even a year before the enactment of the 42nd Amendment, in the *Ziyauddin Burhanuddin Bukhari vs Brijmohan Ram Das Mehra* case of 1975, Justice M. Hameedullah Beg had expressed his confidence in our secular Constitution and democracy. This was a case where the court set aside Bukhari's election to the Maharashtra state legislature on the ground of violating Section 123 of the Representation of the People Act, 1951 since Bukhari had asked Muslim voters to vote for him by exercising undue influence on them.

On the other hand, in the 1995 case of *Dr Ramesh Yeshwant Prabhoo vs Prabhakar Kashinath Kunte*, the court found that an appeal to Hindutva by the Shiv Sena candidate, Prabhoo, did not constitute a violation of Section 123 of the Representation of the People Act. The court held the view that Hindutva was 'a way of life' and refused to accept that Hindutva was a religious ideology. In fact, Justice Jagdish Saran Verma had no qualms about mixing up and using interchangeably terms like 'Hinduism' and 'Hindutva'.

Again, in 1995, in the *Ramachandra G. Kapse vs Haribansh Ramakbal Singh* judgement, the three-judge bench dismissed the contention that the winning BJP candidate from Thane, Maharashtra, Ramachandra Kapse, should be liable for prosecution for corrupt practices under Section 123 of the Representation of the People Act. The petitioner, Singh, had charged that Kapse had been present during the inflammatory speeches of Hindutva leaders and ideologues, L.K. Advani, Pramod Mahajan and Sadhvi Rithambara. The speeches of both Mahajan and Rithambara were held by the court to come under the purview of sub-sections (3) and (3A) of Section 123, and therefore termed as 'corrupt practices'. Since Kapse said, in his defence, that he was opposed to the rhetorical appeal made by speakers like Rithambara, the Supreme Court took Kapse at his word and reinstated him as the winning electoral candidate.

In a high-profile case in the following year, 1996, *Manohar Joshi vs Nitin Bhaurao Patil and Anr*, an election petition was filed in the Bombay High Court by Bhaurao Patil against Manohar Joshi, the winning candidate of the BJP–Shiv Sena alliance. The petitioner alleged the commission of corrupt practices by Manohar Joshi for his alleged statement, 'The first Hindu State will be established in Maharashtra', under sub-sections (3) and (3A) of Section 123 of the Representation of the People Act. The court, in this case, validated Manohar Joshi's nomination on the ground that there was no appeal for votes on the basis of religion, and that, at best, it was an expression of a *hope* to establish a Hindu State in Maharashtra. Interestingly, the validity of this judgement was challenged later by Mohd Aslam (1996 AIR 1611) under Article 32 of the Indian Constitution, which provides a fundamental right to constitutional remedies to all citizens of India. A review or reconsideration of any previous decision is permitted by Article 137 of the Indian Constitution. However, the three-judge bench headed by Justice J.S. Verma unanimously dismissed the civil writ petition in the case.

Clubbed together, these above-mentioned cases are known as the 'Hindutva' cases and primarily deal with the violation of Section 123 of the Representation of the People Act. Sanghamitra Padhy informs us that, in these cases, the petitioners' 'manifest appeals to religion have been redefined [by judges] as appeals to culture or history, oblivious of the context that fosters those appeals. The court thus seems to have appropriated the symbols of Hindu India as Indian culture and history'.[102]

The precursor to the *Hindutva* cases was a crucially important case, which had emphasized the secular nature of the Indian polity. The judgement was delivered by a nine-judge constitutional bench in the 1994 *S.R. Bommai vs Union of India* case, concerning the misuse of Article 356 to dismiss state governments and impose President's Rule. S.R. Bommai, the then chief minister of Karnataka, had challenged the imposition of Article 356 by the Centre on state governments. In this judgement, the court justified its dismissal of BJP-led state governments, following the demolition of the Babri Masjid on 6 December 1992, with the argument that mobilizing votes by using religion amounted to corrupt practice and was against the spirit of the Indian Constitution. Here, the court also reiterated that secularism was part and parcel of the basic structure of the Indian state. In the *Hindutva* cases mentioned in this section, however, the judges hardly considered the reasoning in the *Bommai* case as a worthy precedent to take note of. The exception was the judgement relating to Mohd Aslam's challenge to the *Manohar Joshi* case, where the honourable judges saw no contradiction between their judgement and that of Justice S. Ratnavel Pandian, who had presided over the *Bommai* case.

Of course, not all judges had unambiguous notions concerning the secular character of the Indian polity. In the 1974 case of *St Xavier's College Society, Ahmedabad vs State of Gujarat*, Justice Y.V. Chandrachud, in a rather Westernized vein, had argued: 'The Constitution has not erected a strict wall of separation between the church and the state. We have grave doubts whether the expression, "secular state", as it denotes a definite pattern of relationship, can with propriety be applied to India.'[103] This was a case of the College being concerned about preserving its autonomy in the face of blatant interference from the Gujarat state government. The college, run by Jesuit priests, received grants-in-aid from the state of Gujarat. The Gujarat University (Amendment) Act, 1969, permitted the state government to inspect and control the administration and finances of affiliated colleges, including St Xavier's College.

Ayodhya Babri Masjid–Ramjanmabhumi Case

At times, our learned judges have even changed the definition of secularism as they see fit. In the 1994 case, *Dr M. Ismail Faruqui vs Union of India*, the apex court justified a vision of secularism as having roots in the tolerance of the majoritarian Hindu community and in the Hindu scriptures. This case dealt with the ongoing Ayodhya Babri Masjid–Ramjanmabhumi controversy, and the different judgements in this regard over the past three decades somewhat resemble a rollercoaster ride. Ismail Faruqui had challenged the validity of the Acquisition of Certain Area at Ayodhya Act, whereby 67.703 acres had been acquired in the Babri Masjid–Ramjanmabhumi complex. He also referred to the December 1992 demolition of the Babri Masjid, which had been a place of worship for Muslims, but the court ruled that Muslim worshippers did not really need a mosque to perform *namaz*.

How did this sorry state of affairs come to pass? Our story begins soon after Independence on 15 August 1947. On the night of 22 December 1949, some fifty-odd persons had entered the Babri Masjid in Ayodhya and installed idols of the god Ram. Under normal circumstances, the Uttar

Pradesh government would have arrested the miscreants under Section 145 of the Indian Criminal Procedure Code. Despite stern directives from Prime Minister Jawaharlal Nehru and Deputy Prime Minister Sardar Vallabhbhai Patel to remove the idols, the Uttar Pradesh chief minister, Govind Ballabh Pant, stood his ground and prohibited the removal of the idols, while issuing instructions for the attachment of the mosque. On 29 December 1949, the district magistrate, M. Singh, started permitting daily Hindu prayers with three presiding priests under the dome of the mosque. On 26 April 1955, the Allahabad High Court issued a restraining order on Muslim worshippers, who wished to remove the illegally installed Hindu idols. By 1 February 1986, the mosque had practically turned into a temple full of Hindu worshippers.

As late advocate and human rights activist P.A. Sebastian put it, 'To condone the acquisition of a place of worship in such circumstances is to efface the principle of secularism from the Constitution.'[104] In 1991, the Places of Worship Act mandated that the identity of a religious place of worship as it existed on 15 August 1947, should not be changed. Notwithstanding the existence of such an Act, the demolition of the Babri Masjid on 6 December 1992 was a chronicle of a disaster foretold. Once this happened, the 30 September 2010 Allahabad High Court judgement of handing over the mosque to Ram Lalla could be based 'on the belief that Lord Ram was born under the central dome of the [Babri] Masjid'.[105]

Sebastian explains that if we accept the fact that the Babri Masjid was built by the Mughal Emperor Babar in 1528, the Indian law on this matter is straightforward and quite easily applicable in this case. If one adversely takes possession of a place for 12 years or more, one becomes the owner of the place. This means that the mosque, the Babri Masjid, was the owner of the place where it stood. This was provided by the Limitation Act. There were a few legal suits concerning the Babri Masjid during the British colonial period, but these were all dismissed under the Limitation Act.[106]

The final judgement of the Ayodhya dispute was given by the Supreme Court on 9 November 2019 and went into the question of limitation in some detail. In this case, there were three main parties: Ram Lalla (the deity in infant form), the Sunni Wakf Board, and Nirmohi Akhara, an organization of Hindu ascetics. While doing so, it dismissed the suit filed by Nirmohi Akhara for possession of the disputed site. It, however, upheld the suits of the Sunni Waqf Board and Ram Lalla in the aspect of limitation. While it was clear the suit filed by Hindutva organizations, like the Vishwa Hindu Parishad, on behalf of Ram Lalla had also violated the limitation clause, the judges did not dismiss it.

The disputed land—where once the Babri Masjid had stood—was handed over to the Hindu Trust in charge of building the Ramjanmabhumi temple. The court also ordered the state government to allot five acres, in another place, to the Uttar Pradesh Sunni Central Wakf Board, for building a mosque as compensation for the destroyed Babri Masjid. As far as Hindutva judgements are concerned, the Ayodhya cases would take the top position in that category.

The fallout of the 2019 Ayodhya judgement is that other mosques are now being considered for demolition on the pretext that these were built on sites where temples had been demolished. The Gyanvapi Vishwanath complex in Varanasi is presently at the centre of a new Hindu–Muslim controversy. At the same time, the 1991 Places of Worship Act is facing a slew of challenges in courts across the country. While the focus is on the supposed demolition of Hindu temples for the construction of mosques, little interest is shown in the demolition of ancient Buddhist shrines for the construction of Hindu temples. No doubt, reclaiming Buddhist shrines or Muslim mosques or Hindu temples is an exercise in futility since religious monuments—the world over—are perennially in a state of flux.

Personal Laws

Another major bone of contention is the issue of personal laws, which had been ably defended by religious minority members in the Constituent Assembly. The term 'personal laws' was first introduced in the Presidencies of Calcutta, Madras and Bombay in the late eighteenth century. The Warren Hastings Plan of 1772 made provision for the creation of civil and criminal courts in all districts under British control. The Plan also allowed Hindus and Muslims the right to apply their own personal laws in civil courts. Interestingly, personal laws at that time also included matters related to caste and religious institutions.

The legal system experienced a major upheaval after the Revolt of 1857, but, again, the personal laws were spared, and given the assurance of official non-interference in the personal customs of the natives by Queen Victoria's Proclamation. As Flavia Agnes says, personal laws also underwent changes in the latter half of the nineteenth century: 'While at the initial stage scriptural law was awarded judicial recognition, later on, the British interpretations of the ancient texts became binding legal principles.'[107] So what we call 'personal laws' or 'family law' today could be legal constructions of recent vintage!

It was in the mid-1950s that the Hindu Reform Laws were enacted, despite major opposition from conservative Hindus, and the status of the Hindu marriage was changed from a sacrament to a contract, by introducing divorce and inheritance rights for women. Of course, the reign of patriarchal ideology in family matters continued unabated in the following decades. All personal laws were validated under Article 13(3)(a) of the Indian Constitution which stipulates that 'law' includes custom or usage having the force of law. Personal laws deal with marriage and divorce, maintenance, guardianship, joint family and partition, etc., and find legitimacy in the following:

> Article 13(3). In this article, unless the context otherwise requires law includes any Ordinance, order, bye-law, rule, regulation, notification, custom or usage having in the territory of India the force of law; 'laws in force' includes laws passed or made by a Legislature or other competent authority in the territory of India before the commencement of this Constitution and not previously repealed, notwithstanding that any such law or any part thereof may not be then in operation either at all or in particular areas.

'This stipulation must be read along with Article 372(1),' writes Agnes, 'which mandates that all laws in force immediately before the commencement of the Constitution shall continue in force until altered or repealed or amended by a competent legislature or authority.'[108]

Despite the fact that personal laws were laws in force even in the pre-Hindu law reform period, the judgement in a well-known case in 1951, *State of Bombay vs Narasu Appa Mali*, made claims to the contrary. The Hindu petitioner had challenged the Bombay Prohibition of Bigamous Marriages Act, 1946 on the ground that it violated the provisions of equality and non-discrimination in the Indian Constitution. The petitioner claimed that while monogamy was forced on Hindus, Muslims could have four wives as per their personal law. The honourable judges of the Bombay High Court, Justice M.C. Chagla and Justice P.B. Gajendragadkar, upheld the validity of the Act, but ruled that personal laws were not 'laws in force' under Article 13, as they were based on religious precepts. This judgement attracted much criticism from legal scholars, because the honourable judges failed to distinguish between statutory and non-statutory personal laws and issued a general statement that personal laws were not 'laws' coming under the purview of Article 13. Flavia Agnes points out that, for years, this judgement 'became a stumbling block to test the constitutionality of personal laws, as several courts followed the principle laid down by this ruling, even while examining discriminatory provisions in statutory personal laws'.[109]

The most famous case relating to personal law is *Mohd Ahmad Khan vs Shah Bano Begum* in 1985 in which the Supreme Court gave a verdict granting maintenance to the petitioner, Shah Bano, who had been divorced by her husband in 1978. All divorcees had recourse to Section 125 of the Code of Criminal Procedure, 1973, in order to oblige the ex-husband to pay alimony for the upkeep of the ex-wife and his minor children, if any. While delivering the judgement, Chief Justice Y.V. Chandrachud lamented the fact that the Uniform Civil Code had not been established by law in India, as per Directive Principle Article 44, which enjoins the state to 'endeavour to secure a Uniform Civil Code for the citizens throughout the territory of India'. This comment caused conservative Muslims, especially those in the newly established All-India Muslim Personal Law Board, to protest vehemently, as they wanted the preservation of their personal laws. There were many moderate Muslim voices as well, but these were not effectively covered by the media or given any publicity. In response to the protests by conservative Muslims, the Rajiv Gandhi government enacted the Muslim Women (Protection of Rights on Divorce) Act, 1986, which effectively closed the doors of the courts to Muslim divorcees, who now had to depend solely on their community to enforce their right to alimony. This Act, in turn, led to huge protests by Hindu right-wing ideologues, who condemned what they termed as 'Muslim minority appeasement'. Nearly 35 years later, the Narendra Modi BJP government passed the Muslim Women (Protection of Rights on Marriage) Act, 2019, which criminalizes and deems unconstitutional the triple *talaq* system of instant divorce that was in force in the Indian Muslim community. In effect, both the 1986 and 2019 Acts were passed without any serious discussion with those affected by the legislation, namely, Muslim women.

The accusation of 'Muslim appeasement' against governments by Hindu right-wingers of the Sangh Parivar has been a constant refrain since Independence. In the 1995 case, *Sarla Mudgal vs Union of India*, concerning a Hindu male converting to Islam for reasons of license for bigamy, the honourable judge seemed to be less concerned about gender justice than about religious conversion. Since polygamy was legally permitted to Muslim men, in this case, too, the necessity for a Uniform Civil Code was invoked by the presiding judge. The Narendra Modi government is now considering the possibility of imposing Article 44, or a Uniform Civil Code, across the country.

The top-down imposition of any legislation has always been problematic, since it does not really represent the voice of the people concerned. Over the past few decades or so, voices of women from different religious groups have indeed multiplied and been making their presence felt in public arenas. Women across the board are not asking for a mechanical application of a Uniform Civil Code in their communities. In fact, they are asking for a set of secular and gender-just laws applicable to everyone in the country.

Why is it important to enact gender-just legislation, and at the same time expand their ambit? Women and trans-persons constitute a little over 50 per cent of society. When gendered persons are not categorized on the basis of religion, and they are given equal rights as men, or special rights, secular democracy is deepened. There is some token representation of women in the panchayats and local councils, but not yet in legislatures and in Parliament. The resistance to even modest legislation like the proposed Women's Reservation Bill shows that we have a long way to go in terms of enacting genuine and wide-ranging gender justice. What other such legislation will be tabled and passed in future cannot be foretold, but it needs to be debated intensely by women and LGBTQ groups before being constituted as law by policymakers.

Chapter IV

Deepening Secularism

How does India treat her minority groups? What, in particular, is the status today of India's largest religious minority community, the Muslims?

According to the 2011 Census, Muslims constitute 14.2 per cent of the total population in India, with a population of nearly 172 million. If proportional representation had been given to the Muslim community in the Lok Sabha, there would have been 77 Muslim members of Parliament. Instead, the number of Muslim MPs in the 16th Lok Sabha in May 2014, with the new BJP government of Prime Minister Narendra Modi being sworn in, was merely 22, which was a paltry 4.05 per cent representation of Muslims in Parliament.[110]

Khalid Rahman informs us, 'Ever since Independence, the percentage of Muslim representation in Lok Sabha has never reached...the double digit. Even in 1980, when the representation in Parliament was the highest (49 out of 529) it was less than the actual ratio of Muslims in the population.'[111] The 2006 Sachar Committee Report has amply highlighted the extremely low levels of Muslim representation in government services. In 2006, there were 1.8 per cent Muslims in the Indian Foreign Service, 3 per cent in the Indian Administrative Service, 2.5 per cent in the Indian Railways, 3 per cent in the Home Department, 7.63 per cent in the police force—which, in 2013, had declined to 6.27 per cent.

What is the kind of violence faced by Muslims over the past decade or so? The 28 June 2017 issue of *India Spend* informs us that between 2010 and 2017, there were 63 incidents of cow-related violence, with 98 per cent of these incidents occurring between 2014 and 2017, with Muslims comprising 86 per cent of the victims.[112] When similar statistics are gathered for violence related to triple talaq and love jihad, a more complete picture of the fearful plight of the Muslim community will emerge.

Given the fact that, 75 years after Independence, the socio-economic and political situation of India's largest religious minority is declining steadily year by year, we need to question the relevance of secularism in the polity. In his latest book,[113] veteran journalist Hasan Suroor has come up with a rather astonishing solution to this problem. Suroor claims that Indian Muslims, even at the time of Independence in 1947, had no great love for 'secular'

India, but opted to stay back in the country because of affiliations to land, property and kin. According to Suroor, the so-called secular parties like the Congress have done nothing really to safeguard or promote the interests of the Muslim community. His conclusion is that secularism has failed, and since Suroor equates secularism with the Congress party's ideals, he points out that the Congress has also failed Muslims. Therefore, he suggests, Muslims must look for another pact with the country's majority community, the Hindus. In Suroor's perspective, if most Hindus are committed to the idea of a Hindu Rashtra, then let them establish a state that gives primacy to one religion, Hinduism.

After all, the United Kingdom, where Suroor is domiciled, is also an establishment state, having established the Church of England in 1534. Nevertheless, all religious denominations live peacefully and without discrimination in the United Kingdom today, says Suroor. The establishment of a Hindu Rashtra in India, Suroor adds, in a Hobbesian vein, might lead to more peaceful relations between Hindus and Muslims, who will get some measure of physical security by being subservient to the leaders of the Hindu Rashtra, even if they do not get the abstract right of equal citizenship. Pratap Bhanu Mehta succinctly describes the fundamental features of an ideal state according to the seventeenth-century philosopher, Thomas Hobbes, who had experienced the horrors of the English civil war: 'One of the things we do in setting up a state, Hobbes argued, is to give up the right to private judgement. The sovereign produces order and regularity not only because it possesses a coercive mechanism but also because it is the sole judge of what constitutes a threat to society. Only when we *authorize* the state to make judgements on our behalf can a well-ordered society be produced.'[114]

What is Hobbes's problem of politics? Hobbes famously wrote in Chapter 13 of the *Leviathan* (1651) that the life of a man in a state of nature, when there was 'the warre of all against all', was 'solitary, poore, nasty, brutish, and short'. The only way out is for men to sign a social contract and submit to the will of an absolute monarch or sovereign. The point to note is that Hobbes never limited his notion of sovereignty to monarchy. The sovereign could be one man or an assembly.[115]

Suroor's analogy of the Church of England as the established religion in the United Kingdom and the proposed Hindu Rashtra in India is erroneous, because it obfuscates historical context in both countries. When King Henry VIII cut ties with the Catholic Church of Rome in 1534, because the Pope would not allow him to divorce Katherine of Aragon and marry Anne Boleyn, he established the Church of England as the official and established religion of the nation. Similar developments were taking place in Germany, where a Lutheran state was being established, as protests against the Vatican escalated.

Interestingly, the Anglican Church was bitterly pitted against the Lutheran doctrines in the sixteenth century. By the following century, England was engulfed in long-standing wars with Catholic countries like France and Spain, apart from sectarian conflicts with the Scots and the Irish. The 1648 Treaty of Westphalia brought temporary peace in Europe, but the following year, right in the middle of the English civil war, King Charles I was beheaded by the English Parliamentarians.

The nineteenth century saw considerable progress in terms of the secularization of British society, but the British imperialist state undemocratically continued to subjugate and exploit the people of several countries in Africa and Asia. Imperialism brought about several conflicts even within Europe, because of which European countries have been at each other's throats, at least till 1945. After the terrible toll of violence and loss of life, not to mention ruthless imperialist conquests, we may conclude that the United Kingdom, since the decolonization process of the 1950s, has become a secular state, in spite of holding on to an established religion like the Church of England.

If it took 400-odd years for the so-called establishment state of the United Kingdom to become a full-fledged secular state, following a long process of the secularization of its democracy, do we expect an organization like the Rashtriya Swayamsevak Sangh, which more or less controls the working of the present ruling Bharatiya Janata Party, to adopt a credible policy of toleration towards Muslims and Christians, after 97 years of trying to establish a Hindu Rashtra? A century ago, the well-known Hindu ideologue and later head of the Hindu Mahasabha, Vinayak Damodar Savarkar, had made it clear—in *Hindutva: Who is a Hindu?* —that while Muslims and Christians had their *pitrbhumi* (ancestors' burial grounds) in the Indian subcontinent, they did not have their *punyabhumi* (sacred land) here, as Muslims look to Mecca, and Christians to Bethlehem, as their place of worship. In other words, Muslims and Christians can never really be 'Hindus', which is Savarkar's overarching term for 'Indians'. Considering the exhortations by the Sangh Parivar outfits these days to marginalize, at times even annihilate, Muslims, what kind of physical security can the latter hope for in a Hindu Rashtra? Such a Rashtra would be miles away from Hobbes's idea of a 'well-ordered society'.

Expanding Democracy

Why do even well-meaning individuals and groups in India reject secularism? Part of the reason lies in the fact that Indian secularism is often given a Western tint by defining it solely in terms of the separation between state and religion. As stated in Chapter I, religions in India tend to occupy the public space rather than the private space and call for support and aid from the state. The state, in turn, deems it fit to intervene in religious affairs on a principled, or case-to-case, basis. At the same time, the Indian state is a non-establishment state—that is to say, the state cannot establish a Hindu Rashtra, unless it radically changes several provisions in the Constitution. Furthermore, it broadly adheres to the principle of 'dharma nirpekshata' or state neutrality, whereby the state cannot discriminate between different religions in terms of providing support and aid.

Minority religious groups are more vulnerable to the danger of being engulfed or constrained by majoritarian interests and pressures, and therefore need special protection to preserve their cultural and religious forms of expression. One part of this protection comprises the preservation of personal or family laws for minority communities. This is not to say that gender-just laws cannot be enacted by the state. After all, every religion tends to favour some patriarchal dogma—denial of divorce or reproductive rights to women, dowry demands from the bride's family, clitoridectomy, child marriages, and so on. The problem is with top-down legislation by a state, which refuses to discuss policy measures with the real stakeholders—in this case, the women in each community.

Perhaps the most neglected dimension of secularism is the democratic principle of equality of citizenship (see Figure 2 in Chapter I). If most Indian analysts of secularism tend to emphasize the wall of separation between state and religion, they completely ignore the concept of equal citizenship as a crucial part of any discussion on secularism.[116]

Strengthening democratic practice in any polity is the best way to strengthen secularism. Often, when a country faces a crisis with respect to its secular principles, the reason is usually that the country is experiencing some weakening of its democratic principles.

For example, France has invested in secular principles from the time of the French Revolution. As long as it was a predominantly Christian nation, France did very well as a secular nation. Towards the end of the nineteenth century, the Alfred Dreyfus case, in which a French artillery officer of Jewish background was deliberately falsely accused of spying for Germany, demonstrated the extent of anti-Semitic sentiments in France. But this case also spurred the socialists to pass legislation on the wall of separation between state and religion in 1905, when they came to power in government.

The French Republic is struggling today with the idea of treating its Muslim population on par with its Christian citizens. The demographic profile of France changed somewhat in the 1960s and 1970s, with a large influx of Muslim migrants from the erstwhile French colonies of the Maghreb. Apart from being embroiled in the hijab controversy which began in the late 1890s and continues to this day, France banned the wearing of the burqa for Muslim women in 2011. After the series of coordinated terrorist attacks in Paris in 2015, the vilification of Islam and Islamophobia in France has continued, leading to more threats of violence by what French President Emmanuel Macron calls 'Islamic separatists', but who are actually some extremely alienated French citizens of Arab or African descent living in ghettoes, which are characterized by squalor and deprivation. The inability to take into consideration the aspirations of diverse cultures has led to the present socio-political mess in France. Even though Macron was re-elected as President in April 2022, his closest rival was Marine Le Pen of the openly racist National Rally party.

It indeed took a long time for even the American government to understand that racism was not conducive to democracy. On 11 September 2001, there were four concerted terrorist attacks launched by the Islamic terrorist group, Al-Qaeda, upon the United States of America, in New York and in the Washington, DC area. The USA retaliated by enacting the Homeland Security Act of 2002, and also the USA PATRIOT Act, giving broad powers to law enforcement agencies, without warrants, to invade the privacy of citizens. Official harassment and arbitrary arrests and detention of Muslims followed soon after. The first twenty captives to Guantanamo Bay Detention Camp arrived on 11 January 2002. Twenty years on, as of April 2022, there were still 37 inmates in Guantanamo Bay. Racism and anti-Islamism constitute the biggest threats to America's secular democracy.

Citizenship and Democracy

There is a threat to any democracy if citizens are not treated equally. Citizenship often tends to be a contested terrain in a democracy, and the forms of legal citizenship that were experimented with in the Indian subcontinent during the turbulence of Independence and Partition in August 1947, were entangled with the eruption of Hindu–Muslim violence in both India and Pakistan, and the subsequent decisions of many Hindus and Sikhs to abandon their property to flee from the newly-constituted state of Pakistan for India. The same was the case with the Muslims who fled India, abandoning their homes, in order to migrate to Pakistan. Many of these instances of mass migration were propelled by the fear of violence and the desire for protection from their community and the government. In the first few months after Partition, Hindus and Sikhs were housed in camps within Pakistan, near the Indian border, while Muslims were huddled together in localities within India, near the Pakistan border. The fond hope was that—once the violence in both countries abated—everyone could go back to their homes and property. After all, political leaders in both countries tended to define citizenship according to the English law formula: 'Every person born in the Union or naturalized according to its laws and subject to the jurisdiction thereof shall be a citizen of the Union.'

As early as 24 January 1947, the Constituent Assembly deemed it important to define who could be a citizen of

India. Since all citizens are equal, the Assembly realized that vulnerable groups like religious and social minorities needed special rights, and that these minority rights had to be linked to fundamental rights. The Constituent Assembly therefore set up an advisory committee on minorities and fundamental rights to examine this notion. Are children of foreigners born in India citizens? Are children of parents of Indian descent that are born in foreign countries Indian citizens? The chairman of the committee, Sardar Vallabhbhai Patel, firmly held the liberal view that a person's citizenship should be determined by his or her place of birth (*jus soli*), rather than on claims of descent, ethnicity or blood.

However, the matter became extremely complicated, and had not been resolved even by Independence Day, 15 August 1947. The new conundrum of non-Muslims stranded in Pakistan and Muslims stranded in India introduced a new idea of citizenship based on descent and religious identity. Towards the end of 1948, both Gandhi and Jinnah were dead, and the mass migrations from both sides of the border radically transformed the way of viewing citizenship in both countries. Shortly after, innumerable refugees, with a sense of entitlement and with the connivance of non-state actors like local constables, non-commissioned soldiers, railway guards and ships' captains, began squatting in abandoned property in the two countries. 'It was in response to this quandary that Nehru's government came to a historic conclusion: it had to prevent

Muslim evacuees from returning to reclaim their homes. The "Influx from Pakistan (Control) Ordinance" [was] promulgated in January 1948'.[117] After the 1965 and 1971 wars with Pakistan, Indian Muslims who had migrated to Pakistan came to be formally defined as 'enemies'.

In the state of Assam, a National Register of Citizens (NRC) was prepared after the 1951 Census. This Register was not revised till 2013. Following a Supreme Court order that it should be updated, in Assam, the revised NRC, published on 31 August 2019, conferred Indian citizenship on those who provided evidence that they resided in India before 24 March 1971. Those who could not do so—more than 1.9 million citizens—were seen as illegal immigrants. The decision by the BJP government to apply to the whole of India the revised NRC, as stated by Home Minister Amit Shah in his speech to the Rajya Sabha on 19 November 2019, caused a great deal of confusion and panic and resulted in widespread protests on the ground that the NRC was aimed at depriving Indian Muslims of their citizenship, should they fail to prove their Indian identity.

It took eight years after Independence for the Citizenship Amendment Act (CAA), 1955 to be passed, even though Articles 5–11 in the Indian Constitution define citizenship. The CAA of 1955 provides a much broader definition of citizenship in the Indian context than had been envisaged by Sardar Patel in 1947, by including citizenship by birth, descent, marriage and naturalization. The Act has been amended five times, but it is the CAA of 2019 that has been the most controversial. The enactment of the Citizenship Amendment Act, 2019 has exacerbated the sense of insecurity among Indian Muslims. This Act was expected to fast-track Indian citizenship for persecuted religious minorities (except Muslims) from Pakistan, Afghanistan and Bangladesh. Religious identities had never been a criterion for Indian citizenship and the CAA 2019 changed that by violating the basic principle of equal citizenship in the Indian Constitution. Many people fear that the combination of the CAA and the NRC of 2019 could wreak havoc among India's citizens and strip Indian Muslims of their citizenship. This fear was transformed as a beacon of hope with the civil disobedience movements in at least 14 states in the country, the most famous of these taking place in Shaheen Bagh, comprising mainly articulate and politicized Muslim women of all ages, in the national capital between 2019 and 2020. These movements were forcibly dismantled in March 2020, with the nationwide lockdown during the Covid-19 pandemic.

Deepening Democracy

It might be pertinent to ask why we value democracy.

The word 'democracy' has its origins in ancient classical Greece around 508 BCE, and is derived from two Greek words, *demos* and *kratos*. *Demos* can be translated as 'the people' and *kratos* as 'power', and democracy can be understood as the 'power of the people'. All adult, propertied men could participate directly in policy-making in the *polis* or 'city', and at least one-fifth of the total number of participants were needed at any time in the public assembly for a quorum in order to approve and pass legislation. However, in classical Greece, there were reluctant democrats like Plato (circa 428–348 BCE), who preferred to perceive democracy as 'majority or mob rule'. Plato's disciple, Aristotle (384–322 BCE), never used the term 'democracy', and preferred to characterize the direct democratic participation that prevailed in Athens as 'politics'. Again, while the dominant party of French revolutionaries in the eighteenth century embraced the classical Greek ideal of direct democracy with some dire consequences, the American founding fathers found direct democracy to be unruly and chaotic, and preferred the more tamed and dependable system of indirect or representative democracy, or what they called 'republicanism'.

So, we ask again: why is democracy important? As John Dunn informs us, for the ancient Athenians, the 'point of democracy was the freedom which it made possible'. Dunn goes on to explain the reasons for classical Athens' 200-year love affair with democracy: 'In thinking of freedom every citizen of Athens had a harsh and vivid contrast permanently in mind: the condition of slavery... The public political life of those citizens, the endless seething activity, the myriad independent and unconcerted decisions of its courts and magistrates and public assembly, served not only as external protection or guarantee for that freedom; it also exemplified both their own individual freedom and their collective solidarity in the most graphic fashion every day of every year of the democracy's history.'[118]

In reality, the picture of democracy is neither lyrical nor sanguine. Yet modern constitutional, representative democracies have managed to enforce a general system of the rule of law, which in turn is expected to guarantee the protection of the fundamental rights of citizens. By holding elections regularly every few years, the state is aware that voters will expect some level of accountability from their elected representatives.

A legitimate criticism of democracy is that it works best in modern capitalist welfare economies, rather than in so-called communist states. The reasons are far too complicated and clearly beyond the scope of this chapter. I have thus confined myself to understanding why it is believed that democracy works better in capitalist welfare states rather than in traditional communist states, within the context of secularism. A crucial feature of secularism is freedom of religion, along with special rights for religious minority communities. Many communist states, like the People's Republic of China, have often made attempts to curb the religious worship and practice of all citizens, but especially those of religious minorities, like the 12 million Muslim Uyghurs in the country. This is most unfortunate, considering that communism is also often understood to be a humanist ideology. There is no reason to believe that communism, intrinsically, is incompatible with secularism or with democracy. States need to summon the will to create improvised and practical solutions to the great problems of the day, instead of holding on to past practice.

Concluding Remarks

On 15 August 1947, India became an independent democracy, which entailed two principles—one, popular control over collective decision-making, and two, equality of rights for all citizens in the exercise of that control. While it is true that we have fallen short of both these principles from time to time, we have survived somehow as a functioning democracy for over 75 years, against all odds and in spite of the forecast of doom and destruction of Indian democracy doled out by many influential people around the world at the time of our Independence. As a people, we continue to struggle to retain our fundamental rights in a nation-state that is unable to shake off caste hierarchies and communal tension. But democracy is not an all-or-nothing matter; it is a matter of small, incremental steps towards the final goal which may never be realized in full measure. It is a goal worth reaching, however approximately, because democracy can provide the values of liberty, equality and non-discrimination to its citizens, especially to lower castes and classes, who are more involved in the political process of voting than any other group.

In the context of secularism, liberty or freedom of religion, including the freedom to believe or not to believe, is of crucial importance in India. In other words, the state should provide equal protection to religious believers and to agnostics or atheists. The values of equality and non-discrimination are important, both for religious and secular matters. The state should not discriminate against any religion or intervene in religious affairs, except on the principled basis of providing support and aid, when required by religious institutions, and for correcting financial and legal lapses on their part. There should be special provisions for vulnerable religious minority groups as a form of protection against brute majoritarianism. At the same time, the state should take steps to ensure that all citizens are treated equally in matters other than those pertaining to religion, and also provide special rights to historically sidelined groups like Scheduled Castes and Scheduled Tribes.

The following are the main features of the secular state in India, as enshrined in the Constitution:

a) The state does not establish any religion and therefore may be considered a non-establishment state.

b) The state broadly follows a policy of 'dharma nirpekshata' or non-discrimination with respect to all religions, both aiding and supporting religious institutions and intervening in religious practices on a principled basis.

c) Freedom of religious worship and practice is accorded to all religions, and the freedom for non-believers is guaranteed. Special provisions are made by the state to protect religious minority groups against the brute force of the majority.

d) Equality of citizenship, the bulwark of democracy, is guaranteed to all; at the same time, a few vulnerable minorities like Scheduled Castes and Scheduled Tribes are given differential citizenship in the form of reserved seats in legislatures, education and services.

It seems to me that these are constitutional provisions that are worth preserving and fighting for, by all citizens of this country.

Suggested Readings

Acevedo, Deepa Das, 'Secularism in the Indian Context', *Law and Social Inquiry*, vol. 38, no. 1 (Winter 2013), pp. 138–67

Agnes, Flavia, 'Personal Laws', in *The Oxford Handbook of the Indian Constitution*, edited by Sujit Choudhury, Madhav Khosla and Pratap Bhanu Mehta, Oxford University Press, 2016

Bajpai, Rochana, 'Minority Representation and the Making of the Indian Constitution', in *Politics and Ethics of the Indian Constitution*, edited by Rajeev Bhargava, Oxford University Press, 2008, pp. 354–91

Bhargava, Rajeev, 'India's Secular Constitution', in *India's Living Constitution*, edited by Zoya Hasan, E. Sridharan and R. Sudarshan, Permanent Black, 2002, pp. 105–33

___, ed., *Secularism and Its Critics*, Oxford University Press, 1999

Bilgrami, Akeel, *Secularism, Identity, and Enchantment*, Harvard University Press, 2014

Brown, Vivienne, 'The "Figure" of God and the Limits of Liberalism: A Rereading of Locke's Essay and Two Treatises', *Journal of the History of Ideas*, vol. 60, no. 1 (January 1999), pp. 83–100

Chandhoke, Neera, 'Individual and Group Rights: A View from India', Hasan, Sridharan and Sudarshan, eds, *India's Living Constitution*, pp. 207–41

—, *Beyond Secularism: The Rights of Religious Minorities*, Oxford University Press, 1999

Chatterjee, Joya 'South Asian Histories of Citizenship, 1946–1970', *The Historical Journal*, vol. 55, no. 4 (December 2012), pp. 1049–71

Dhavan, Rajeev, 'Religious Freedom in India', *The American Journal of Comparative Law*, vol. 35, no. 1 (Winter 1987), pp. 209–54

Dunn, John, ed., *Democracy: The Unfinished Journey, 508 BC to AD 1993*, Oxford University Press, 1992

Heredia, Rudolf C., 'Secularism in a Plural-Religious Society: The Constitutional Vision', *Economic and Political Weekly*, vol. 50, no. 14 (4 April 2015)

Hobbes, Thomas, *Leviathan*, 1651

Holyoake, George Jacob, *Christianity and Secularism*, London, 1863

Jha, Shefali, 'Rights versus Representation: Defending Minority Interests in the Constituent Assembly', in Bhargava, ed., *Politics and Ethics of the Indian Constitution*, pp. 339–53

Kesavan, Mukul, *Secular Common Sense*, Penguin, 2001

Locke, John, *A Letter Concerning Toleration*, 1689

Luthra, Ved Prakash, ed., *The Concept of a Secular State and India*, Calcutta: Oxford University Press, 1964

Mahajan, Gurpreet, 'Religion and the Indian Constitution: Questions of Separation and Equality', in Bhargava, ed., *Politics and Ethics of the Indian Constitution*, pp. 297–310

Mehta, Pratap Bhanu, 'Passion and Constraint: Courts and the Regulation of Religious Meaning', in Bhargava, ed., *Politics and Ethics of the Indian Constitution*, pp. 311–38

Needham, Anuradha Dingwaney, and Rajeswari Sunder Rajan, eds, *The Crisis of Secularism in India*, Orient Blackswan, 2009

Padhy, Sanghamitra, 'Secularism and Justice: A Review of Indian Supreme Court Judgements', *Economic and Political Weekly*, vol. 39, no. 46–47, pp. 5027–32

Pantham, Thomas, 'Indian Secularism and its Critics: Some Reflections', *The Review of Politics*, vol. 59, no. 3 (Summer 1997), pp. 523–40

Prasad, Ganesh, and Anand Kumar 'The Concept, Constraints and Prospect of Secularism in India', *The Indian Journal of Political Science*, vol. 67, no. 4 (October–December 2006), pp. 793–808

Rahman, Khalid, 'Indian Secularism and Religious Minorities', *Policy Perspectives*, vol. 14, no. 2 (2017), pp. 35–53

Rajan, Nalini, *The Story of Secularism: 15th–21st Century*, Authors Up Front, 2016

Sebastian, P.A., 'Secularism and the Indian Judiciary', *Economic and Political Weekly*, vol. 45, no. 50 (11–17 December 2010), pp. 42–45

Sen, Ronojoy, 'Secularism and Religious Freedom', in Choudhury, Khosla and Mehta, eds, *The Oxford Handbook of the Indian Constitution*, pp. 885–902

Stephens, Robert J., 'Sites of Conflict in the Indian Secular State: Secularism, Caste and Religious Conversion', *Journal of Church and State*, vol. 49, no. 2 (Spring 2007), pp. 251–76

Suroor, Hasan, *Unmasking Indian Secularism: Why We Need a New Hindu–Muslim Pact*, Rupa, 2022

Thapar, Karan, 'HC Misunderstood SC's 1954 Verdict, Wrongly Applied Essentiality Test', *The Wire*, 17 March 2022

Thapar, Romila, *Somanatha: The Many Voices of a History*, Penguin, 2004

Vanaik, Achin, *The Furies of Indian Communalism: Religion, Modernity, and Secularisation*, Verso, 1997

Verma, S.L., 'Reformulation of Indian Secularism', *The Indian Journal of Political Science*, vol. 46, no. 1 (January–March 1985), pp. 32–48

Yildrim, Seval, 'Expanding Secularism's Scope: An Indian Case Study', *The American Journal of Comparative Law*, vol. 52, no. 4 (Autumn 2004), pp. 901–18

Endnotes

1 Edited by James Hastings (New York, 1954), p. 347.

2 The 'disenchantment of the world' is a term popularized by the sociologist Max Weber (1864–1920), to describe a rationalized world where the effect of religion in everyday affairs is mitigated, and individuals in society feel alienated and find little meaning in life.

3 George Jacob Holyoake, *Christianity and Secularism* (London, 1863); citation on p. 35 of S.L. Verma's 'Reformulation of Indian Secularism', *The Indian Journal of Political Science*, vol. 46, no. 1 (January–March 1985), pp. 32–48.

4 John Locke, *A Letter Concerning Toleration* in *7 Works*, Kindle edition, p. 4538.

5 Ibid., p. 4813.

6 Ibid., p. 4993.

7 Ibid., p. 4921.

8 See Chapter 1 of Nalini Rajan's *The Story of Secularism: 15th–21st Century* (Authors Up Front, 2016).

9 Rajeev Bhargava draws a distinction in the present day between a state which establishes one religion and a

theocratic state. While a theocratic state, like the Islamic Republic of Iran or Taliban-ruled Afghanistan, is governed by religious laws directly administered by a priestly order, the establishment state of the Anglican Church in England, or the Roman Catholic Church in Italy and Spain, or the Evangelical Lutheran Church in Sweden, have created conditions for religious tolerance and non-discrimination, without necessarily following the dogma of separation of state and religion. See Bhargava's 'India's Secular Constitution', in *India's Living Constitution* edited by Zoya Hasan, E. Sridharan, R. Sudarshan (Permanent Black, 2002), pp. 105–33. In Locke's time, however, there was no real difference between the theocratic state and the state which established one religion. When a particular religion was established, there was no freedom or equality as far as the other religions were concerned.

10 Rajeev Bhargava, ibid., p. 107.

11 See pp. 92–93 of 'The "Figure" of God and the Limits of Liberalism: A Rereading of Locke's Essay and Two Treatises' by Vivienne Brown, *Journal of the History of Ideas*, vol. 60, no. 1 (January 1999), pp. 83–100.

12 Article 29(2): No citizen shall be denied admission into any educational institution maintained by the state or receiving aid out of state funds on grounds only of religion, race, caste, language or any of them.

13 Bhargava, 'India's Secular Constitution', p. 110.

14 Ibid., p. 117.

15 K. Santhanam, *Constituent Assembly Debates* (hereinafter *CAD*), volume VII, 6 December 1948. The debates are

available online (see https:/www.constitutionofindia.net/constitution-assembly-debates/).

16 *CAD*, volume VII, 6 December 1948.

17 The numbering of the clauses given here is as mentioned during the debates in the Constituent Assembly. These may not correspond exactly to those in the report submitted on 13 April 1947. The numbers of the various clauses kept changing as the debates went on. In fact, as late as November 1949, a few members pointed out errors in the final numbering of the articles and sub-clauses. It is only in the final document of the 1950 Constitution that the numbering was fixed, so to speak.

18 *CAD*, volume V, 30 August 1947.

19 See pp. 275–76 in 'Sites of Conflict in the Indian Secular State: Secularism, Caste and Religious Conversion' by Robert J. Stephens, *Journal of Church and State*, vol. 49, no. 2 (Spring 2007), pp. 251–76.

20 Ibid. Vishwambhar Dayal Tripathi wanted cow protection to be a fundamental right. It finally appeared as a directive principle (non-justiciable) as Article 48 in the Indian Constitution.

21 Cited on pp. 793–94, 'The Concept, Constraints and Prospect of Secularism in India' by Ganesh Prasad and Anand Kumar, *The Indian Journal of Political Science*, vol. 67, no. 4 (October–December 2006), pp. 793–808.

22 *CAD*, volume VII, 2 December 1948.

23 *CAD*, volume VII, 8 November 1948.

24 *CAD*, volume VII, 3 December 1948.

25 Gurpreet Mahajan, 'Religion and the Indian Constitution:

Questions of Separation and Equality', in *Politics and Ethics of the Indian Constitution*, edited by Rajeev Bhargava (Oxford University Press, 2008), p. 304.

26 Penguin Books, 1981, revised edition, p. 19.

27 Ibid., pp. 569–70.

28 Ved Prakash Luthra (ed.), *The Concept of a Secular State and India* (Calcutta: Oxford University Press, 1964), p. 202.

29 *CAD*, volume VII, 8 November 1948.

30 *CAD*, volume VII, 3 December 1948.

31 *CAD*, volume VII, 15 November, 1948.

32 See p. 5027 of Sanghamitra Padhy, 'Secularism and Justice: A Review of Indian Supreme Court Judgements', *Economic and Political Weekly*, vol. 39, no. 46–47, pp. 5027–32.

33 Cited on p. 527 of Thomas Pantham's 'Indian Secularism and its Critics: Some Reflections', *The Review of Politics*, vol. 59, no. 3 (Summer 1997), pp. 523–40.

34 Rudolf C. Heredia, 'Secularism in a Plural-Religious Society: The Constitutional Vision', *Economic and Political Weekly*, vol. 50, no. 14 (4 April 2015), p. 53.

35 See p. 539 in Thomas Pantham, op. cit.

36 For a more complete analysis of Gandhi's distaste for any interface of state and religion, see T.N. Madan's 'Whither Indian Secularism?', *Modern Asian Studies*, vol. 27, no. 3 (July 1993), pp. 667–97.

37 Madan, ibid., p. 676.

38 Pantham, op. cit., p. 539.

39 'Gandhi's Secularism', *Proceedings of the Indian History Congress*, 2009–2010, Volume 70, pp. 1124–33.

40 Ibid., p. 1125.
41 Ibid., p. 1128.
42 Ibid., p. 1129.
43 Ibid., p. 1132.
44 Accessed online from 2–22 April 2022. Here are a few extremely useful analyses of these debates: Shefali Jha's 'Rights versus Representation: Defending Minority Interests in the Constituent Assembly', in *Politics and Ethics of the Indian Constitution*, edited by Rajeev Bhargava (Oxford University Press, 2008), pp. 339–53; Rochana Bajpai, 'Minority Representation and the Making of the Indian Constitution', in Bhargava, ibid., pp. 354–91; Gurpreet Mahajan, 'Religion and the Indian Constitution: Questions of Separation and Equality', in Bhargava, ibid., pp. 297–310; Neera Chandhoke, 'Individual and Group Rights: A View from India', in *India's Living Constitution*, ed. Hasan, Sridharan and Sudarshan, pp. 207–41.
45 Chandhoke, ibid., p. 211.
46 Jha, 'Rights versus Representation: Defending Minority Interests in the Constituent Assembly', p. 343.
47 *CAD*, volume V, 27 August 1947.
48 Ibid., 28 August 1947.
49 Ibid.
50 Ibid.
51 Ibid., 27 August 1947.
52 See Rochana Bajpai, 'Minority Representation and the Making of the Indian Constitution', p. 372.
53 Ibid., p. 374.
54 See note 17.

55 *CAD*, volume III, 1 May 1947.
56 Ibid.
57 Ibid.
58 Ibid.
59 *CAD*, volume VII, 7 December 1948.
60 Ibid.
61 *CAD*, volume V, 30 August 1947.
62 *CAD*, volume III, 1 May 1947.
63 *CAD*, volume VII, 7 December 1948.
64 Shefali Jha, op. cit., p. 349.
65 *CAD*, volume VII, 7 December 1948. The actual modification had been made by the Drafting Committee, while examining the Report of the Advisory Committee on 1 November 1947.
66 For a more comprehensive analysis, see Neera Chandhoke, 'Individual and Group Rights: A View from India', pp. 215–16.
67 Jha, op. cit., p. 344.
68 *CAD*, volume V, 28 August 1947.
69 Jha, op. cit. See pp. 344–45 for a more comprehensive discussion on the subject.
70 *CAD*, volume V, 28 August 1947.
71 *CAD*, volume VII, 3 December 1948.
72 *CAD*, volume VII, 8 November 1948.
73 *CAD*, volume VII, 4 January 1949.
74 Ibid.
75 Ibid.
76 Jha, op. cit., p. 345.
77 *CAD*, volume VIII, 25 May 1949.

78 Ibid.

79 Ibid.

80 Jha, op. cit., p. 339.

81 *CAD*, volume X, 14 October 1949.

82 Bajpai, op. cit., p. 355.

83 *CAD*, volume VII, 8 November 1948.

84 See Rajeev Bhargava's Introduction in *Politics and Ethics of the Indian Constitution*.

85 *CAD*, volume XI, 25 November 1949.

86 See p. 5028 of Padhy, 'Secularism and Justice: A Revies of Indian Supreme Court Judgements', for this citation.

87 See p. 912 of Seval Yildrim's 'Expanding Secularism's Scope: An Indian Case Study', *The American Journal of Comparative Law*, vol. 52, no. 4 (Autumn 2004), pp. 901–18.

88 See p. 899 of Ronojoy Sen's 'Secularism and Religious Freedom', in *The Oxford Handbook of the Indian Constitution*, edited by Sujit Choudhury, Madhav Khosla and Pratap Bhanu Mehta (Oxford University Press, 2016), pp. 885–902.

89 The rationale for the Hindu Religious & Charitable Endowment Act, 1951, is that the Act exists for better administration, protection and preservation of temples and the endowed properties attached thereto, and for fulfilment of the objects, with reasonable restrictions, which do not violate the rights of religious freedom guaranteed by the Constitution.

90 For an excellent analysis of this case, see Ronojoy Sen, op. cit.

91 Rajeev Dhavan, 'Religious Freedom in India', *The American Journal of Comparative Law*, vol. 35, no. 1 (Winter 1987), pp. 209–54.

92 Karan Thapar, 'HC Misunderstood SC's 1954 Verdict, Wrongly Applied Essentiality Test', *The Wire*, 17 March 2022.

93 Article 14 reads: 'The State shall not deny to any person equality before the law or the equal protection of the laws within the territory of India.'

94 Citation by Rajeev Dhavan and Fali Nariman in Ronojoy Sen, op. cit., p. 893.

95 It should be noted that the idea of taxing the huge finances of a religious institution by the state does not contravene Article 27, which states: 'No person shall be compelled to pay any taxes, the proceeds of which are specifically appropriated in payment of expenses for the promotion or maintenance of any particular religion or religious denomination.'

96 See pp. 152–53 in Deepa Das Acevedo's 'Secularism in the Indian Context', *Law and Social Inquiry*, vol. 38, no. 1 (Winter 2013), pp. 138–67.

97 'Harijan' or the 'children of Hari' is how M.K. Gandhi referred to untouchable castes.

98 See Ronojoy Sen, op. cit., pp. 894–97, for an excellent analysis of the repercussions of describing Hinduism as 'a way of life'.

99 Ibid., p. 897.

100 For a fuller, albeit more critical, survey of cases regarding minority rights, see K. Vivek Reddy, 'Minority Educational

Institutions', in *The Oxford Handbook of the Indian Constitution*, pp. 921–42.

101 See *In Re: The Kerala Education Bill, ... vs Unknown on 22 May, 1958* (1959 1 SCR 995).

102 Padhy, op. cit., p. 5029.

103 Ibid. See p. 5028 for a more comprehensive account of this case.

104 See p. 43 of 'Secularism and the Indian Judiciary' by P.A. Sebastian, *Economic and Political Weekly*, vol. 45, no. 50 (11–17 December 2010), pp. 42–45.

105 Ibid.

106 Ibid.

107 See 'Personal Laws' by Flavia Agnes, in *The Oxford Handbook of the Indian Constitution*, p. 905.

108 Ibid., p. 909.

109 Ibid., pp. 909–10.

110 See the excellent analysis of this issue by Khalid Rahman, 'Indian Secularism and Religious Minorities', *Policy Perspectives*, vol. 14, no. 2 (2017), pp. 35–53.

111 Ibid., p. 42.

112 Cited in ibid., p. 44.

113 Hasan Suroor, *Unmasking Indian Secularism: Why We Need a New Hindu–Muslim Pact* (Rupa, 2022).

114 Pratap Bhanu Mehta, 'Passion and Constraint: Courts and the Regulation of Religious Meaning', in *Politics and Ethics of the Indian Constitution*.

115 *Leviathan*, Chapter 26, 'Of Civil Lawes'.

116 Neera Chandhoke's *Beyond Secularism: The Rights of Religious Minorities* (Oxford University Press, 1999), is an

illustrious exception to this trend. However, Chandhoke believes that it is important to go *beyond* secularism in order to strengthen the democratic principle of equality and ensure that vulnerable minorities are protected from brute majoritarianism. I hold the view that the democratic principle of equality is a precondition and a part of secularism, which is defined as a triple-value system, as described on in Chapter I of this book.

117 For further elaboration of these points, see pp. 1063–64 in Joya Chatterjee's 'South Asian Histories of Citizenship, 1946–1970', *The Historical Journal*, vol. 55, no. 4 (December 2012), pp. 1049–71.

118 See p. 242 of Dunn's 'Conclusion' in John Dunn (ed.), *Democracy: The Unfinished Journey, 508 BC to AD 1993* (Oxford University Press, 1992).